A SEASON IN SPAIN

ANDREW *and* LESLEY
GRANT-ADAMSON

❦ A SEASON IN SPAIN ❦

ANDREW *and* LESLEY GRANT-ADAMSON

PAVILION

First published in Great Britain in 1995 by
Pavilion Books Limited
26 Upper Ground
London SE1 9PD

Designed by Nigel Partridge

A CIP catalogue record for this book is available from the
British Library

ISBN 1–85793–305–2

Phototypeset in Palatino by Intype, London
Printed and bound in Great Britain by
Butler & Tanner Ltd, Frome

2 4 6 8 10 9 7 5 3 1

This book may be ordered by post direct from the
publisher. Please contact the Marketing Department. But
try your bookshop first.

CONTENTS

For John and Mary Puddefoot

CHAPTER ONE

THE HOUSE
BY THE RIVER

FOR A SEASON we lived in an olive grove in Spain. We went looking for a house and were beguiled by a tiny fruit farm near an Andalusian river. Beneath its ancient olive trees thrived acres of oranges, lemons, peaches, almonds, quinces and loquats. Fig trees shaded the house and vines dripped from its terrace. We found it in summer.

'It's the romantic option,' we warned each other, 'not the sensible one.'

But the sensible one was withdrawn once we had taken the sensible decision. The romantic option became the only one.

It rained the day we moved in. Summer had become December. Eager to put customs and confusion behind us, we had driven through the night from the ferry port at Santander. The roads were empty. Villages fled by in a landscape of moonlit monochrome. We drove fast and free, and when we crossed the Sierra Morena that cuts off Andalusia from the rest of Spain, it began to rain.

In Granada we sought breakfast in a bar by the railway station. The waiter was taciturn, the city dull as any on a rainy Sunday morning. Drizzle hid the Alhambra and the snowy mountain peaks beyond. We hurried on south, to the Alpujarra.

This is the rocky world where the Moors settled when they were chased out of Granada five hundred years ago. They are very much in evidence, especially in the clusters of flat roofed houses that might be taken for villages in north Africa; and in the irrigation system that waters the terraces. Our olive grove was on the fertile river plain of the Guadalfeo, twenty miles from Granada as the eagle flies and twelve miles from the Mediterranean.

In summer the *camino*, the dirt road from the main road, had been yellow dust billowing in the breeze. On the day we moved in, rivulets criss-crossed its surface. We parked where a slender path, a mule track, joined it and we began to walk. For the first few yards we skirted a field and then we were beneath olive trees. The track meandered. We had to hop over irrigation channels and several times we paused to look up to our left, high up to the snow on the mountains. The air was sweet and clear, and very, very cold.

Then the path began to drop and we saw our house. It looked different: in the summer only one stretch of its patio had been covered and now it all was. Before, the first glimpse had been of the curving wall of the dining-room with its stained glass window. Now the new roof jutted into view ahead of it. A pity, we thought, that this had spoiled the line. But as we stood beneath its cover that wet morning we did not imagine there could be any other disadvantages to it.

The house was a long, low L-shape with a flat roof of *launa*, a grey shale. When the owner, an English-woman we'll call Sally, acquired the property the previous summer, there was only a typical local *cortijo*, or farmhouse: a row of four or five rooms, each opening on to a strip of paving. Some of them had been living accommodation and the rest used for animals or storage. The old house leaned against the bank. In a flurry of activity, this building had been turned into kitchen, dining-room, bedrooms and bathroom. Then a new wing had been built to provide a large sitting-room and bedroom. A sinuous passage linked the two areas. Eight doors opened on to the patio.

The house was full of beautiful touches, some original and some traditional Spanish. A window in the passage shed golden light because it was not a window of glass but of stone the colour of amber. The centre bar of a window in the new bedroom was curved, to echo the shape of the olive tree a few yards away. Small blue tiles were dotted at random among the heavy dark clay ones of the indoor floors and the patio.

Everywhere, white walls set off dark beams in Spanish style. Some ceilings were made of cane in the local manner. A vine was growing from a trough in the dining-room and in a few months was to arc across the beamed entrance to the kitchen. Terracotta bowls were used as washbasins in the bathroom and kitchen. The bathroom was a fantastic creation of blue and white tiling, a muddled dream of the Moorish and the Oriental. All that could be said with certainty was that it had what the French call a *toilette à la Turque* and which the Spanish do not discuss at all.

Sitting on the patio the previous summer, drinking tea in the fluttering shade of an orange tree, we had talked about crops and animals. Of course, have the crops, Sally said; and yes, keep goats, a few chickens, whatever we fancied. Later we made plans for the crops but ruled out the animals. Animals limit travel. We knew Spain a little but not well and this was our best chance to see it. But we wanted the crops. Olives would pay well, and health food shops in London would be delighted with an offer of the other fruit, organically grown, assuming the regulations allowed us to send them our produce.

We offered to look after Sally's cat. Although we had never had anything to do with cats, one would be useful in fending off less welcome animals.

'And the dog?' she suggested.

'OK, the dog too.'

But, in the shilly-shallying days between summer and December, the dog went to expensive quarantine in England. Sally rang to tell us, and to say, 'I'm leaving you a silky young tabby called Cosmo.' She added instructions about chasing off a big cat, from a neighbouring *cortijo*, that came marauding whenever Cosmo was fed.

Cosmo seemed desperate to be fed the morning we arrived. She squeaked and scampered and danced about on her hind legs and did everything but shout at us that she was starving. Unversed in the ways of cats, we believed her and, as soon as we had the key to the house in our hands, opened a packet of cat food. There was plenty of cat food. A dozen packets were lined up on the shelf in the dining-room.

That array of cat food rankled once we looked around. Things that should have been provided for *us* were nowhere to be found. Although the house had beds for six or seven, it was barely equipped for four. Furniture and furnishings noted in the summer had vanished.

But explorations were cut short by the arrival of a large black cat who edged Cosmo from the feeding bowl. We chased it off, and over the next half hour took turns to stand on guard. The black cat was brazen. It might have been joined to the feeding bowl by a length of elastic, it rebounded so persistently. In a while we let it win, too busy to do otherwise. There were possessions to ferry in a wheelbarrow along the mule track, damp rooms to air, and we had to launch a serious search for means of heating. No, there was no time to be firm with a thieving cat. That would have to wait. And when we had done it all, and when we had discovered cleaning materials and begun to attack the muddy paw marks that covered every surface a paw might reach, well it was then that we came upon the note. Sally's note, saying she had left us her black cat called Posy, and here was some ointment to put on her temples.

The black cat called Posy regarded us stiffly and would not let us near.

Early next morning a bird sang in the darkness. A while later oranges glimmered through half-light. The new day was dry and sharp, the colours brilliant as only the coldest weather can make them. Indoors it was colder. Glaze on pottery mugs crackled as hot tea was poured into them. Those terracotta wash-basins chilled water before we could wash and the two-bar electric fire gave little more heat than a candle. We were cast back to childhood memories of unheated houses with frost inside windows. If it did nothing else, our time in the Alpujarra would remind us what the seasons were like.

Strolling through the olive grove we took stock. There were nine olive trees, huge ones, the biggest measuring more than eighteen feet around the trunk. There were 135 orange trees of several varieties, three lemon trees, and perhaps half a dozen almonds . . . But the paths curved and were incomplete, we doubled back and lost count and then realized we had not included trees on the lower land. This was a narrow terrace reached by ducking beneath the washing line and risking a headlong plunge. After the rain the path was slippery, but it was down there that we earmarked land for our vegetable patch.

We gave up counting trees and walked to the edge of our land. Between us and the river lay a few neglected terraces with olive trees blackened by fire, and a tumbled farmhouse. Across the river rose the Sierra de Lújar, 6,000 feet of rounded, gently folded Triassic limestone with a scattering of buildings abandoned when they stopped mining fluorspar. It was bare, except for an almond grove, perhaps an acre, teetering on a crag above the river.

Behind us soared western Europe's second highest mountain range, the Sierra Nevada, its ragged outline peaking at 11,421 feet at Mulhacén, which we could not see, and topping 10,000 feet on the Loma de Cáñar which we could. On the lower slopes were white villages, a scattering of tawny farmhouses and the deep green of olive groves.

CHAPTER TWO

NEIGHBOURS

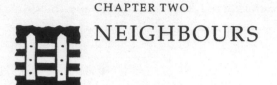

WHERE THE MULE TRACK joined the *camino* there stood
a simple *cortijo* where a quick little man with a big
smile grew beans and lettuces and raised a few
chickens. When he wore his straw hat with the down-
turned brim he looked like a merry gnome. Antonio
was a small farmer in every sense. He did not reach
five foot in height and his farm was no more than a
few terraces of olives and oranges, a field where poppies blazed in springtime, and the fenced vegetable
plot in front of his house. The fencing, high and unat-
tractive chain link, was an innovation. Traditionally
all land had been open, with everyone free to walk
anywhere.

On the face of it, all that had changed over the
centuries was that some people had fenced their vege-

tables against the peripatetic herds of goats. With Antonio sitting in the sun, his back against the white-washed wall of his house, we were looking at a snap-shot of the timeless Alpujarra.

But the camera lied because at dusk Antonio locked up and returned to his home a mile away on the main road where he lived with his family. It was the modern pattern. Like the men on neighbouring farms, who walked out from the flats in the town, he came each morning to tend the land his family had worked for generations, and then he went away again. At week-ends wives and children and grandchildren came out. They sat around and admired the crops and scenery and thoroughly enjoyed it all, just as long as they did not have to live there any more.

Antonio let us park our jeep by his gateway so that we did not block the *camino*. It was convenient for us and he felt it made his house appear occupied at night and reduced the risk of theft. He had a number of alarming stories about men like himself finding tools or crops had vanished under cover of darkness. And he had once lost his own chickens that way. He told these stories in an accent that managed to sound harsh and slurred all at once. The speech of the Alpu-jarra has taxed the descriptive powers of every writer who has ventured near it, and one cannot better the suggestion that it is like water pouring from a jug. Words are smudged together in a gurgling, tumbling rush. The *montañero* speaker has no love of consonants and so lets them fall silently from the ends of syllables. The final 's' he ignores altogether. But offer him a 'c' or a 'z', which the Castilian speaker lisps into vari-ations of the English 'th', and the man of the Alpujarra will twist it into an 's'. If he can get hold of a 'j', he does his utmost to make it a clattering 'k'. He is no admirer of vowels either . . .

We listened to Antonio's stories and took our cues from the smiles that broke over his face, and hoped we laughed in the right places. Friends in London had warned us that it would be difficult to learn Spanish in the Alpujarra but we had not appreciated the extent of the difficulty. What we were going to pick up was the equivalent of, say, a thoroughgoing Geordie accent with dialect to suit.

Like all the country people we met, Antonio had three favourite topics of conversation: the weather, and other people's money and fecundity. The first time we spoke to him he asked how many children we had – None? Well, there was still time – and he asked how much rent we paid. Startling in the early days, this directness was to become so familiar we ceased to notice it.

Antonio was not our nearest neighbour. From deep among the olive and orange trees, somewhere beyond the giant fig tree that overhung our flat roof, we heard voices. A man sung a moaning, repetitive line of song as he worked. Women's voices joined in conversation. Now and then someone was called, the caller's voice thrown so that it travelled out across the terraces, the final vowel of the cry loudest and long. The stretched sound lingered, echoing. But usually what we heard was the soft murmur of Spanish among the trees. It is a good language for murmuring among trees.

Each day the crowing of a cockerel wakened us, a ginger cat slunk around the end of our house to watch us. Somewhere, close but invisible, were neighbours.

We climbed the outside steps to the roof terrace above our bedroom, and looked for them through the fig tree's tangle of winter-bare twigs. But we could see nothing of our neighbours. No flash of lime-washed walls, no wisps of smoke. Instead we saw the purest white of snow on the high peaks; sunshine painting the folds of mountains; lofty olive trees whose branches chopped the sky into segments of blue; and below us a drift of orange trees. Black caps tic-tic-ticked among the foliage, the yelps of little owls made us start, and we heard the murmuring of Spanish. But we could not find our neighbours.

Early one Sunday morning there was shooting, so loud that we realized the man with the gun was practically outside our bedroom window. Was this the singer of the sad song? As the bedroom window had neither shutters nor curtains, we did not leap out of bed to make his acquaintance but sank beneath thick felted Spanish blankets and muffled our ears against his noise.

One day, three chattering women came round the end of the house, short nut-brown women of indeterminate age, wearing black except for the muted colours of scarves tied over greying hair. With much smiling, they begged permission to use our patio as a short cut.

'We've been gathering wild fennel,' they explained, holding out samples of damp green fronds for our admiration.

It occurred to us that the newer part of our house had been built across a mule track, one of the multitude that link the farms. Neighbours would not lack other routes, but why should they give up this one? It was the tradition to walk anywhere one chose.

We shifted chairs to let them through, gesturing for them to continue. '*Pase. Pase.*'

They walked slowly past each room, exclaiming as they took in the features. The eccentric bathroom stopped them dead. Their babble of dialect required no translation. In any language, it was an astonishing bathroom. This was a room that merits a description, not merely because of its strangeness but because it was locally famous. By the time we knew it, it had already become a motif for the excesses of foreigners. There were two doors to it, an ordinary one from an adjoining bedroom and another from the patio. The patio entrance, with double doors half-glazed and fitted with shutters, stood open whenever the room was not in use because that was the only means of airing it.

It was large, about twelve feet square, with a tiled floor the colour of baked red earth. Against the rear wall to the right was the lavatory, up two steps to bring it level with the top of the bath that ran along the rest of the wall. Above the pan rose an arched recess of blue, white and red tiles of Moorish design. The water tank was on the roof, the 'chain' from it an ornately tasselled cord which seemed to have escaped from the drawing-room of a Victorian country house. The whole thing was like a throne, if you can imagine a king squatting on the edge of his throne because he was afraid of a mouse.

By contrast, the bath was conventional although the width of its blue and white tiled surround was such

that it led each set of house guests down similar con-
versational byways.

First visitor: 'How did *you* get into the bath? My
legs weren't long enough, I had to balance on the
ledge and lower myself in.'

Second visitor: 'Oh, I moved a flower pot off the
side of that other bath so I had a step.'

Then they compared manoeuvres for climbing out.
There were ingenious solutions to the problem of average length limbs and extra wide spaces.

'What,' they all demanded to know, 'is Sally like?'

We confessed we had spent more time looking at
her house than at her. They pieced her together for
us. She was extraordinarily short, or how else explain
the low sinks that made us all bend at the knee when
we used them, and the position of mirrors in bedroom
and bathroom? She was extraordinarily tall, or how
else explain the gymnastics involved in getting in and
out of the bath?

But this, remember, was the conventional bath. The
other one, set at right angles to it and hedged about
with pots of ferns and succulents, was the curiosity.
It was much smaller, a deep tiled trough where one
could crouch and scoop water over oneself. The water
supply trickled down a cascade of grey stones set into
the wall. None of our visitors admitted to using this
bath. For one thing, they would have faced the
open-mouthed interest of a tank of tropical fish on
the shelf at one end.

Finally, there was a terracotta washbasin with a tiled
surround, the whole shaped like a washing boiler with
a place beneath for the fire. We often wondered how
visitors described that bathroom to their friends. No

wonder our fennel-picking trio were stopped in their tracks when they reached it.

Few of the people who came to the house saw the second bathroom; the very concept was a blow to modesty. Open to the world, it was half-circled by a stone wall a foot high. Within was another lavatory to squat at and a stone tank to scoop water from. The soap dish was a scallop shell set into the wall. A screen of cane gave minimal protection and privacy. Flowers and vines grew all around. And the view was stupendous, across to the river and up the valley to the mountain where the sun and the moon rose.

'I like to be close to nature and my children respect my privacy,' Sally had told us when she showed us this bathroom. Our neighbour Maria never alluded to it, although we sometimes met her close by as she scurried across our land. It was a while before we discovered exactly where she lived, this smiling, gap-toothed woman who appeared and was gone before we had time to phrase more than a greeting. We had seen her over here and over there, therefore she must live in that direction. But did she? From the roof terrace there was still no evidence of neighbours.

Maria did not need an exotic bathroom to bring her close to nature. She lived the kind of life her family had done for centuries, and it had weathered her face and shaped her. Early during the olive harvest we met her properly and then the mysteries, of the invisible *cortijo* and the owners of the voices that we heard soft as a breeze, were dispelled.

With a cry of '*Hola!*' she appeared suddenly beside us and begged olive cuttings for her goat. At the first hiss of a *si*, she whisked out the rope country people seem always to have concealed about their bodies. In seconds she had swept together a great mound of leafy twigs, lashed them together, hoisted them on to her back and, uttering enthusiastic thanks, was away. From behind she was a mobile shrub propelled by a pair of black-shod feet.

We grabbed lesser bundles and, having no handy ropes coiled around our waists, staggered after her with arms full, eager not to miss this chance of discovering how people managed to pop up close to us without warning. Our route took us behind the new wing of our house and then down to a terrace, the usual mix of olive trees protecting orange trees.

It was difficult to keep up, Maria was fast and we were unsure of our footing. A very few terraces away we came upon her *cortijo*. In a direct line, it was about a hundred yards from where we were living. But it had not been made fancy, toyed with and turned into something for which it was never intended. A blue plastic bucket standing outside was the only evidence that we had not walked back centuries.

Maria seized the goat in one hand and the bucket in the other, and squatted down in the doorway to milk. Hens scrabbled in a dung heap. The cockerel we heard each morning, a white one, looked on and a ginger cat slithered by. Maria's bundle of olive cuttings had been tossed aside, on to a pile of fodder. We added ours.

Between pulls on the goat's teats, she introduced us to her husband and his sister, and the husband introduced us to his mule. A domed oven of whitewashed stone stood outside the house. 'Do you ever use that?' we asked.

They laughed, that would be old-fashioned. 'No, we keep hens in it now.'

Like everyone else, they bought their bread from the baker who delivered it by putting loaves in the cloth bags hung from trees along the lanes, the nearest his van could get to the scattered farmhouses.

One of the women wondered aloud about our children and our rent. We changed the subject. 'What is the name of your *cortijo*?'

'Los Frailes,' they replied. But we had been told Los Frailes, 'The Friars', was the name of ours. We asked what they thought ours was called. The reply sounded like 'Cortijo Joachin' but we were having enormous difficulty with the local accent and could not be certain. It would not have been surprising if they were applying a personal name to the property because a great many houses and pieces of land are known by people's names. Their first names. Among those we came to know was a house called Tio Mateo, Uncle Matthew. Very few houses display names on written signs, and people's surnames are as seldom used as house names. You simply ask: 'Where is the house of Mari Carmen?'

One of the delightful things about life in the Alpujarra is that people are not reduced to street numbers or, at the post office, to box numbers. Letters addressed simply with an approximation of our names and the word 'Órgiva' reached our mailbox safely. Andrew rapidly became Andrés, because the local response to foreign names is to convert them into Spanish equivalents. Lesley proved untranslatable and was therefore called nothing. Her middle name, Ann, would have done nicely because then she would have become Ana, but we did not think of that in time to use it. Sometimes names are altered for other reasons than awkwardness in pronunciation. A Danish man we came to know was quite happy to be known by a translation of his surname, rather than by his first name which, quite absurdly from the Andalusian point of view, was Ole.

Renaming intrigued us. Popes and members of royal families are translated into Spanish while entertainers, writers and politicians are not. Thus it happened that television schedules announcing the broadcast of a British-made programme called 'Elizabeth R' had to explain in brackets 'Isabel 2'.

So there we were, a lengthy walk down a mule track from the nearest traffic, with a handful of unobtrusive neighbours hidden among the trees. Quiet. Remote. A peaceful place to write without distraction, to learn about our youngish citrus trees and our ancient olives, and to make the transformation from London life to the slower rhythms of the countryside. The essence of tranquillity? Mmm, we thought so too.

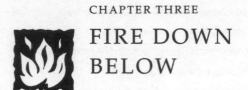

CHAPTER THREE

FIRE DOWN BELOW

DAYS WERE WARM under the December sun. We sat outside, with the thermometer hovering around the seventy Fahrenheit mark, and lunched on garlicky salads of local vegetables washed down with freshly-squeezed orange juice from our own trees. But that was when the sun was high. After it sank behind the mountains, nights were bitter.

Although the early-morning cold was fearsome, and rooms did not retain the previous day's heat, by ten-thirty we were tearing off layers of clothes and opening shutters and generally being hustled from one climate to another. At about five in the afternoon the heat disappeared and we lit fires, three in this sprawling house. Whoever was on fire duty got jolly warm indeed scampering up and down the terrace flinging kindling about. Whoever was *not* grumbled that each fire smoked unless it was accompanied by a knife-thrust of draught from an open window. By that time, of course, our clothes were many layers thick again and scarves were a good idea.

We discovered the disadvantage of the new patio roof: it prevented the sun reaching several rooms and kept them cold and dark. Neither Maria's *cortijo* nor Antonio's, nor any of the others along the *camino*, were protected in that way. Instead they grew vines that give shade in summer and die back to nothing in time to let in the winter sun.

And so wood was ordered, logs for the woodburning stove we did not possess. Otherwise, we were warned, we would get tree trunks. Then we set about modifying the fireplace in the living-room, raising the fire bed and using a board to reduce the height of the opening. We did not entirely stop it smoking but we were no longer kippered every time we put match to wood.

Posy watched the improvements with her green-eyed gaze and returned to her chair on the patio. This was where she spent most of her days, looking like a black fur glove someone had dropped there. She was still refusing the ointment but, in any case, her temples seemed fine. It was the crusty grey patches on her ears that suggested something was not quite right.

Apart from our further attempts with the ointment, only two things disturbed her lolling: food and the realization that someone was on the way to the washing line. A trip to the line was a signal for Posy and the young tabby, Cosmo, to wrap themselves around ankles, Posy purring and Cosmo, who seldom purred, making excited squeaks. We never worked out what they imagined would happen, unless their weaving around our feet resulted in one of us falling headlong to the lower terrace, which was a distinct danger.

We went out to buy a fan heater, all the way to Granada where we expected the hypermarkets to offer a greater range than our local town. They did, but the biggest selection was of silver painted flying saucers. Those we did not understand.

Home again, we switched on our precious fan heater and the lights went out. Every time we tried to use it at more than half power the circuit breaker cut our electricity. And even at half power it went off if we switched on the electric kettle. It was impossible to have a fire on, do the ironing and listen to the BBC World Service all at the same time. And this in a four bedroomed house, with Christmas and three guests only days away! Fresh from centrally-heated city homes, our visitors would expect indoor comfort as well as Spanish sunshine, and this house was more difficult to heat than a Victorian rectory. We shouted for help.

Help was Manolo, the electrician. One night there was a knocking on the door of the sitting-room and we found a lightly built man eager to explain. Unfortunately, those hours of learning Spanish from tapes and books had done nothing to prepare us for discussing the intricacies of lighting and power circuits.

Manolo had wired the house when it was a shell. Afterwards the builders had made changes. His ready explanations petered away. Slowly he worked things out. The sight of the bathroom amazed him but he rallied quickly and rather doubtfully said *bonito*, pretty. Inspecting the socket above the washbasin he declared it to be for power. To us it had looked like a light socket, although the only way to turn the light off was to remove the bulb.

We had been tricked in the kitchen too. It had seemed obvious to plug the kettle into the only socket above the work surface. But this, Manolo proved, was for lights. The single kitchen power point for appliances was behind the sink.

'I didn't know where they were going to put things,' he said, rolling his eyes and shaking his head in the internationally accepted manner of people in the building trade when talking about the work of others.

Worse was the news that we had only 2.2 kilowatts of electricity, the standard basic supply. If you have more, the standing charge is higher. For conservation it is a great idea, for keeping warm it is not. We would never be able to use more than one bar of the fire and the lowest level of the fan heater at the same time. To boil a kettle we would have to switch one of them off.

Walking back to the *camino*, Manolo pointed out with pride the metal pylons he had erected for the cable carrying our paltry supply. They looked fit to carry power to a village.

Two nights later, at half-past nine, the arrival of the firewood was announced by four men clamouring at the sitting-room door. Their lorry was on the *camino* and that was where they dumped the load, half on the road and half on a neighbour's strawberry patch. One of them brandished a piece of wood, seeking agreement that it was indeed chopped small enough for a stove. Then they drove off.

'We'll have to move it now. We're not going to stay friendly with the neighbours if the *camino* is blocked in the morning,' said Andrew. Luckily, it was a beautiful night, an almost full moon lighting the mule track and silvering the snows of the high peaks. There were falling stars and a nightingale.

After the first few trips with the wheelbarrow the joy waned. Not only was it exhausting work, Andrew pushing the barrow and Lesley stacking the logs, but we had discovered why the load had been delivered at night. Many of the logs would hardly fit in an inglenook fireplace, let alone a stove.

About one in the morning we broke off. We had shifted half the wood and made space for a car to pass between Antonio's gate and our pile. By eight we were back at work. Antonio looked knowingly at the giant logs when we mentioned how late they had arrived. To lighten the mood Andrew recited an English proverb: 'He who chops the wood gets warm twice.' Antonio's face creased into a smile and he capped Andrew's with an incomprehensible Alpujarran one about black pudding, *morcilla*.

No one had warned us about the cold. 'I want to be somewhere warm in winter for once in my life,' Lesley had said. We did not realize olives and oranges need what horticultural books call 'days of cooling'. We thought that their presence signified year-round warmth, not more frosty nights than we were used to in London.

The mind remembers what it chooses to. Neither of us then recalled what Gerald Brenan had written in

22

South from Granada about trying to ward off the cold during his stay in the Alpujarra in the 1920s. But in any case, the village where he lived, Yegen, was higher, 3,400 feet above sea level, and exposed. We were about 1,500 feet and deep in a valley. Now we returned to the book. Brenan had rejected traditional Spanish home heating, preferring to add fireplaces and create a cosy area behind heavy curtains.

We, too, had rejected *braseros*. Those electric flying saucers we had seen in Granada and Órgiva were up-to-date versions of the heaters that fit into the bases of the round tables, *mesas camillas*, found in every Spanish home. A heavy tablecloth is thrown over the table and the family sits there, tucking the cloth around their laps as they would a travel rug.

In villages, and the poorer parts of towns, wood-burning *braseros* are still in use. We often saw people in the streets knocking out yesterday's ashes and lighting new fires in the shallow metal dishes, twigs flaring up and left to die down to smouldering embers that could be taken indoors. It is normal while walking through an Alpujarran village on a winter day to have to step around someone's *brasero* or for a flash of flame to catch the eye as a black-clad woman down an alley puts the match to that evening's fire. Usually the women do this chore.

Spain was once a country covered by forests but the ravages of sheep and goats, and man trying to keep warm during savage winters, have made wood scarce. The *mesa camilla* was a way of economizing: an armful of twigs kept a whole family cosy for an evening.

Perhaps it explains the placidity of the Spanish. Half

a dozen people around a table, no more than a yard across, cannot afford violent emotions. To leave the table is to be cold. If you are becoming excited or angry a Spaniard will pat you on the shoulder and say *'Tranquilo,'* calm down. Given our limited power supply, we resisted buying an electric *brasero* but we succumbed to a tablecloth woven in the traditional Alpujarran style in stripes of red, brown, cream and gold. When it was exceptionally cold we slipped the fan heater under the table.

And we learned to be careful. We nearly set fire to the home of Francisco and Begoña. Like us they were *forasteros* – people from outside – although Begoña had come from no further than Granada and Francisco was from Barcelona. They had moved to the Alpujarra to open the first optician's shop in the town and a pharmacy in a village.

We were sitting around the *mesa camilla*, in their flat above the pharmacy, drinking coffee. Begoña started to sniff the air and we all smelled overheating plastic. Lesley had not tucked the cloth around her and her knees had pushed it towards the electric *brasero*. The plastic undercloth was starting to soften. After that incident we were meticulous about tucking ourselves up in the approved manner. But our most alarming experience was in a bar. We had become used to bars and restaurants providing *braseros*, frequently their only form of heating, so when the motherly woman who cooked us lunch bobbed out of the kitchen to offer us a fire we said yes, please. To our horror she wheeled over a large gas fire, lit its jets and shoved it beneath the tablecloth with us, making sure the fabric was snugly covering the safety vents.

CHAPTER FOUR

WHITE CHRISTMAS

QUIET. Remote. The essence of tranquillity? Not quite. We returned from our first foray to find a young English family stripping one of our few ripe orange trees. The man was wearing a cheeky grin and a hat that put us in mind of Eddie Grundy of 'The Archers'.

'What are you doing?' Silly how one asks the obvious.

'Sally said we could have a bag of oranges.' We were to become used to hearing what Sally said.

Their bag was a full-sized sack. When it was brimming, the man went straight to where our wheelbarrow was concealed and swung the sack on to it, ready for the journey down the mule track to their vehicle. His wife looked around for the two children. They were investigating one of the precious mandarin trees.

'Don't you have oranges where you live?' The obvious again.

The wife said that no, they lived too high up. She described a *cortijo* a few kilometres along a track above one of the white villages we could see from our roof. 'We have chestnuts instead.' They enthused about the wonderful quality of their chestnuts.

Chestnuts were in season too. We like chestnuts and we know several delicious things to do with them. We angled for some chestnuts. 'We swap do we? Our oranges for your chestnuts?'

'Oh no,' they said in unison. She looked again for the children. He took a step towards the wheelbarrow.

The Grundies were first of a succession of the uninvited visitors, and in a number of ways they were typical. They shuttle between England and their *cortijo* in the Alpujarra. They are knowledgeable about the region and love it deeply, for the life it offers them and for its breathtaking beauty. With this goes respect for the local people and their way of living that is adapted to climate and terrain. We seldom encountered a trace of that superiority born of ignorance that often marks the Britisher abroad.

Two days after we met the Grundies, we came home to discover another young couple from England starting our olive harvest for us.

'What are you doing?'

'Sally said you didn't want the crops. She said we could have them all.'

We said, 'Oh no you can't,' and then struck a deal

with them. Knowing nothing of olives, we had planned to enlist experienced help and this couple, organic
farmers with their own diminutive farm a mile or
two away, seemed a practical choice and required no
persuasion. Immediately, it turned out that it was too
early to begin on the harvest and we ought to leave
it until after Christmas. The man folded their net, the
woman discarded their sticks. They went away.

Day after day we were roused by cries of *'Hola!'* as
unexpected visitors appeared on our patio. All were
North Europeans, living Grundy-like lives up in the
mountains, some in tents. There were long dresses
and long hair and vague long-winded conversations
during which they would occasionally ask for work,
always ask whether Sally had left anything for them,
and then recommend a particular bar in town. We
said that yes we would look in there some time, and
determined to avoid it.

Flicking their eyes around they invariably spotted
something they said belonged to them. Someone
declared ownership of Andrew's green wellies. Someone laid claim to an olive net, which was actually a
pile of our fly screens. There were numerous attempts
on a motorbike left by the hedge and repeated
requests for its key, which we did not have anyway.
Always they went away empty-handed, although in
some hearts hope sprang eternal and they rebounded
on us. They seldom came as individuals: whole families or groups of friends descended on us. Their dogs
rampaged, chasing Cosmo and Posy up trees. We gave
up being politely dissuasive and became downright
discouraging. They continued to come.

But what were they all doing in the valley anyway?

27

We had known the Órgiva area for a number of years and were taken aback by this influx. One of our reasons for choosing the Alpujarra was that it was essentially Spanish rather than cosmopolitan. Behind our backs this part of it had changed. Why? Well, Órgiva is the spiritual centre of the world. When someone made this rather large claim in a magazine, he opened a floodgate to New Age people from northern Europe. The idea still has currency: we groaned when we heard a British composer interviewed on the BBC World Service talk about a great ley line crossing the Alpujarra. His remark would surely result in a further wave of astrologers, herbalists and masseurs; another cluster of tepees poking up from the wooded terraces; a further dilution of the Spanish culture.

Other people came because they were interested in experiencing that Alpujarran culture. One of the most frequent questions we faced was, 'Have you read the book?' By this they meant Brenan's *South from Granada*. Yes, we had. We were numbered among the hordes who made their first sorties into the Sierra Nevada because of that book. Not that Brenan or any other writer had a kind word for Órgiva, it was merely a point on their journeys between more interesting places.

A different set of people came to the valley by chance, attending courses at a centre for alternative studies. The outstanding beauty of the scenery and the possibility of a calmer, simpler life led them to abandon careers in favour of the alternative rigours of living closer to the land in a tough climate.

Mid-life escapees, new-style hippies or people of

the book, it was not easy to pin down the attraction the place held for them. After all the verbiage they ended up murmuring that it just felt like a good spot to be.

The Alpujarrans seem less confident of the inherent goodness of the place. They must spend more on fire crackers and rockets to frighten away evil spirits during fiestas than the people of any other bit of Spain. The sound resembles warfare more than devotion: sometimes the barrage echoes around the mountains all night while a statue is paraded through stumbling alleyways between white-painted houses.

Órgiva itself is one of those towns that guide books describe as: 'The gateway to . . .' It is a practical town, living for its present, not its past. Most things you need are there: a good selection of shops, banks, a post office, bars and several restaurants.

A Moorish-looking palace, a sorry brick pile, stands on the corner by the traffic lights. Its ground floor has become gloomy shops – greengrocery and hardware. Posters advertising circuses or competition nights at local discos are flyposted on its walls. Above the building crumbles a squat square tower that retains a semblance of dignity. There were plans to turn the palace into a folk museum and restaurant but, while we were there, there was no more progress than with the more important local schemes: a reservoir, and a by-pass for the town. What did happen was that other old buildings were demolished to make way for additional shops, offices and blocks of flats.

When we arrived there were three supermarkets; not large shining palaces of consumer choice but village shops with open shelves and tally books at the check-outs. Meat and vegetables were served from behind counters but with little finesse. We bought pork chops and the puzzle of the splintered bones in restaurant meals was explained. A hand axe, the kind used for chopping wood, was swung down on the meat. Chickens were quartered the same way. It was inelegant but not ungenerous, because when we bought a choice piece of chicken they followed the custom of donating one of the less useful pieces of the bird.

A weekly market used to be held in a square in the heart of the town but, shortly before we arrived, it was moved. Now it takes place on an arid patch by the bed of the dry river, the Rio Chico, that skirts the town. Dwindling numbers of country people bring baskets of fruit, vegetables and herbs to the Thursday market and sit, black-clothed and patient. Alongside them are the stalls of gypsy vegetable traders with the richer choice from the coast. Next to them, the gaudy stalls of Africans touting junk jewellery, cheap radios and clocks.

A shoe stall sets out its wares, a display of goods from the factories of Spain, Italy and South America. From a hook screwed into the end of the stall hangs a tangle of *campesinas*, the local sandals that lace around the ankle. For centuries their soles were woven esparto grass, now they are old tyres. We bought soft Spanish leather shoes for going out and *campesinas* to wear around the *cortijo*. Mule tracks are tough on footware.

We had to learn to count again. How much were the tomatoes? 'Twenty *duro*.' A *duro* is five pesetas and in practice it is the basic currency unit. In shops and supermarkets, whatever was registered on the till, it was normal to carry out a transaction to the nearest *duro*. Sometimes you gained a couple of pesetas and next time you lost them.

Needing extra bedding for our Christmas visitors, we returned to the department stores and hypermarkets of Granada. There we developed our theory of the essential difference of nations. While everyone in Europe eats the same deep frozen pizzas, drinks the same brand of beer, wears the same fashions and watches the same films on television, there remains one variation. Difference re-asserts itself at night and its symbol is the pillow. The British hug soft oblongs, the French hard bolsters, and the Germans fluffy squares shaped with a karate chop. No doubt this says something profound about national character-istics.

The Spanish pillow is a sausage, softer than a French bolster and designed to fit the complete width of a bed. Our beds were futons, not Spanish mattresses. In the hypermarkets we pulled dozens of pillows from the stacks. None fitted our pillowcases. Eventually we accepted they would stick out of the ends. Later, though, we succeeded in buying a Spanish pillowcase locally, in the nearest thing Órgiva has to a department store, a clothes and drapery shop on the corner of the square.

'We would like a sixty centimetre pillowcase, please.'

After disappearing into the hinterland, the assistant produced a box. In it was *the* pillowcase. There was no other. A fine pillowcase it was too, with a zip instead of a flap to stop the pillow popping out. We took it, there was no choice.

The plaza where this shop stands is in reality a wide main street. Beside the twin towered church a woman has been shoehorned into a newspaper kiosk. She bobs there, like a jolly Judy, delving out of sight to find what her customers request. Andrew became a regular, using *El País* as an aid to learning Spanish. Until a few years ago there were central islands with orange trees but these were ripped out, apparently to ease the way for traffic.

Pavements were widened and a row of bars set out tables opposite the church so that customers can be entertained by the traffic jams. So too are the knots of old men who idle away their days there, playing dominoes or cards but rarely buying a drink. The chairs are used as freely as park benches. Only at the height of the summer tourist season might a waiter spring forth anticipating that you want something to eat or drink.

If parking rules were enforced, the road would be wide enough. There were plenty of police in the town: the *Policía Local* in their navy uniforms, and the national *Guardia Civil*, green garbed and still, when posing outside their barracks, wearing their distinctive patent leather hats. Caged partridges hung on the wall of the barracks. An oblique warning to miscreants perhaps? Occasionally, the navy blue police rushed around issuing parking tickets but mostly they waited until everything was jammed and then made a desultory effort to sort out the muddle. Fortunately the locals are obliging drivers. Rarely was a horn blasted in anger.

Inside one of the bars opposite the church Andrew once waited more than two hours to meet our visitors,

32

drinking the quarter-pint glasses of beer called *cañas* and eating *tapas*. By custom these little snacks are provided free with alcoholic drinks. But it is more complicated than that. They may be handed out only between certain hours and only with particular drinks. Bars vary in their practice, and of course the quality of their *tapas* varies too. The customer makes no selection, eating whatever arrives. The most common offering is a slice of cheese or local ham on a piece of bread, but practically any of the local dishes may be served up in minute quantities. As Andrew found, during his long wait while our guests trundled up from Málaga airport, a customer who stays for several drinks can work his way through a range of snacks.

On Christmas Eve we, who are not regular churchgoers, and Marsha, who is not Christian but likes to experience all a country has to offer, went to midnight mass. The service was simple, without Angelus bell or incense. Haunting folk tunes were played on *laúdes* and *panderos*, Andalusian versions of the lute and tambourine. The congregation sang with such gusto that a member of a charismatic Anglican congregation would not have felt out of place.

The church was being renovated and redecorated. Its twin towers were built in the eighteenth century in imitation of those of the basilica of Nuestra Señora de las Angustias in Granada, but the building dates from the sixteenth century. The Órgiva retable is a magnificent golden baroque concoction. In the centre of the ornate screen is the town's treasure, a carving of Christ on the cross attributed to Juan Martinez Montañes, one of the greatest Andalusian sculptors.

From the late sixteenth century polychromed wood

was the favoured art form of Spain. Montañes, the first of the Seville school of sculptors, was known as 'The God of Wood'. With a Protestant suspicion of idolatry, we were slow to appreciate the power and beauty of Andalusian religious carving. Most of the pieces remain in churches to be venerated, rather than being removed to galleries to be regarded as art.

After we had celebrated the birth of Christ and were ready to trail out into the starry night, the congregation moved forward and formed a queue at the altar rail. Curious, we followed them to the front. The priest was cradling a statue of the Holy Child in his arms, worshippers kissing the baby's raised knee. Between kisses, he wiped the knee with a muslin cloth. After the simplicity of the demystified service, the scene was unexpected, a breath of something ancient and mysterious.

Christmas morning was crisp and bright. As the sun rose we drank steaming coffee on the patio and made plans for the day. We decided that in one respect it would be an English-style Christmas, with presents opened around a log fire. That meant waiting until evening, not long compared to the Spanish who hold out until the Feast of the Three Kings on January 6. On that day, presents for Órgiva's children are handed out on the church steps in the happiest of religious festivals.

Lesley and our visitors drove up to Cáñar, 2,000 feet above us by twisting roads, for the view over the valley and away to the sea. Cáñar is not on the tourist route. There is nowhere beyond it unless you are willing to risk the springs of your car, and there is nowhere for tourist buses to turn. They call the village

'The Balcony of the Alpujarra' and that is what it is, sitting on a spur over 3,400 feet above the distant Mediterranean. Other villages are higher but they hang on the sides of valleys, their views restricted.

Cáñar is a perfect harmony of townscape and land-scape. Both seem naturally ordered. Steep cobbled alleys thread between flat, *launa*-roofed houses unchanged in design since the arrival of the Berbers. Animals are kept on the ground floors, chickens, goats and mules peer out into the brighter light.

That Christmas morning, there was a decorated tree beside the octagonal fountain in the square. People gathered to talk in the sun. Outside the bar with its spectacular views to the east, Cáñar was already thinking of its fiesta of the Music of the Lasses. A man with a guitar was practising the traditional songs young lovers sing on December 28. One of them goes likes this:

You are more beautiful, lass,
Than the snow lying in the hollow,
Than the carnation in a glass
And the lily in the meadow.

Marsha, who came originally from New York, regarded it as a highlight of her holiday that she was serenaded in a Spanish village on Christmas morn.

Back at the house Andrew had been cutting logs for the evening, squeezing oranges and cooling a bottle of *cava*. He had also prepared food for the barbecue.

The barbecue was bucolic. A hefty rock served as a table with smaller rocks for chairs. Similar stones ringed the inside of the concrete pool near it, disguis-ing it as a rock pool. Unfortunately, that leaked.

Over smouldering olive twigs, we roasted peppers and aubergines, and grilled prawns alongside two delicious staples of the Alpujarran diet: rich *chorizo* sausages and *morcilla*, known to us as blood pudding or black pudding. While the pieces were being turned and the tantalizing smells wafted through the olive grove, we mixed our *cava* with orange juice and celebrated the day with bucks fizz.

That evening we dined on a delicately flavoured *bonito*, a fish of the tuna family, bought on Christmas Eve in the fish market at Motril on the coast. We cracked almonds from our own trees and ate them with dried muscatel grapes from Málaga.

It was a Christmas for basking in sunshine, marvelling at magnificent scenery, and eating fresh and flavoursome food, most of it produced within a few miles of our table. And of course it was a white Christmas. We had only to look up and there was a thick white Christmassy layer on the Sierra Nevada. We decided to go and play in the snow.

As the road zig-zagged the mountainside, we left behind the vivid orange trees and then the olives at around 3,250 feet above sea level; then at 4,500 feet we rose above the wintering cherry trees, apples and chestnuts of the Poqueira valley. Hairpin bends lifted us up higher and higher through pine forest until we emerged above the tree line at 8,000 feet. The snow line was still hundreds of feet above us, demonstrating that it was another of the winters the Alpujarra dreads, a winter with scant snow to water the land in summer. To call it a snow *line* makes it sound a neat demarcation. Here you have snow and there you have stunted brittle grass. But you don't. Here you have occasional patches of snow and when you get over there you also have occasional patches. We parked the car a few hundred feet above where Andrew had spotted the first blob.

There were grey rocks jutting against a blue sky, thin yellowish grass of a mean spikiness, and a breath of ice in the air. The snow around us steamed in the sun, the vapour whisked away by intermittent breeze and then rising again, quite distinct against the clear sky. And it seemed the purest cleanest snow any of us had ever seen, untainted by emissions from factory chimneys or traffic fumes. Snowballs? But we could not. The snow looked fluffy but it was diamond hard, resisting scraping or chipping let alone being gathered into balls for mock battle.

We climbed a few feet higher and up on to a big rock, exhilarated by the thin pure air. Fingers tingled, pains shot through heads so we abandoned walking in favour of a discussion of altitude sickness. How had Olympic athletes coped in, say, Mexico when we could not stray more than a hundred feet without feeling something seriously amiss? Lesley's finger was swelling around her wedding ring. For a while we sat, needing to recover from our minimal exercise. Mountain range after mountain range rolled away below us, summits golden green and flanks shadowed in purple. We saw the scattered coastal towns, saw ships like dark hyphens on the sea, and we saw the Rif mountains of Morocco.

CHAPTER FIVE

OLIVE HARVEST

THE OLIVE HARVEST began with a rattle. The sound spread through the adjoining *cortijos* and we knew it was time to start gathering our own crop.

There is no mechanization to help. In the Alpujarra olives are picked the way they have been since the Romans introduced them to Spain 2,000 years ago. The rattle was the sound of long canes, *cañas*, being tapped against branches to shake the fruit tree. Nets are laid on the ground to catch the olives. Trees are vast and gnarled from centuries of pruning – no machine could shake them. Even if they were smaller, machines could not travel along the mule tracks to reach the narrow terraces. We studied the tree outside our bedroom window and speculated about the Moor who probably planted it.

The deal we had struck with the young English organic farmers, Patrick and Barbara, was that we would all share in the work but when it was done they would have cash from the olive mill and we would take our portion in oil, enough to last out our time in Spain. Barbara had cast her soft brown eyes over our trees and hazarded a guess at what they might yield.

Our harvest began the morning Patrick arrived on horseback with a net. We selected a tree and spread the net. Then we chose canes from a pile left over when the patio roof was lined. Tentatively we struck our first blows at the branches where the olives dangled. They pelted down like shards of jet.

But what looked decorous and gentle when we saw our neighbours harvesting, turned out to be harder work in our case. Our trees had been poorly tended for years. Patrick swung up into the tree, wellington boots grinding on bark as he struggled to keep his balance while slashing out with an axe at the dead branches that impeded our canes. Olives rained on us, pinging on skulls, stinging exposed flesh, and bouncing into the net and out again. Our blackest and best flew into the undergrowth yards beyond the net, and Lesley discovered it was to be her job to go ferreting after them. Neither of the cats had ever seen an olive harvest before and thought it was a great game. They tangled in the net, frisked after bouncing olives and carried them away to play with. Posy was being kittenish but the grey patches on her ears had turned into red lumps she would not let us investigate. When Patrick came down to earth we showed him.

'Ticks,' he said, and gave a demonstration of the classic way to remove a tick: hold the animal firmly, hold the tick even more firmly and twist clockwise to remove the anchoring legs as well as the engorged body. Then he burned the tick with a match, before it could damage another animal or human. Tick fever is an unpleasant complication of country life.

By dusk, when goat bells signalled the approach of the peripatetic herd across the abandoned land, we had harvested 100 kilos of olives. Many more had been lost in our golden carpet of oxalis or Bermuda buttercups, and because our land was rutted. The Spanish keep the ground beneath olive trees flat and bare as an earth floor. They want rain to penetrate the soil quickly and reach roots, rather than sustain greenery. Also, it makes it easier for them to gather up olives which fall naturally before harvest or miss the net.

Olives which do not land in the net can be collected in three ways. The modern method is to use a machine that resembles a lawnmower without blades. A spiked roller impales the olives which are then caught in a basket. No one suggested a name for this machine, an odd omission as not all farmers owned them and much borrowing went on. 'What do they ask for?' we wondered. On flat ground fruit is swept up with dustpan and brush. The third way is to sit on the ground and pick them up individually. On rough ground, this is the only way.

We used the machine-without-a-name on the few patches of our land where it was suitable but most of the work was done by hand. Perhaps there is something therapeutic about picking olives from the ground and putting them in a plastic bucket. It certainly was not financially rewarding. A great many olives went to make up a kilo which sold to the mill for the price of a cup of coffee.

Lesley liked to go out early in the morning and pick up olives, and it was Antonio's favourite way too. He sat there for hours at a time to gather half a bucketful, a tiny figure who was quite easy to miss unless we spotted the movement of his hat. But he was always happy to take a rest to talk and smoke a Ducados, the strong black tobacco cigarettes so popular in the country. Occasionally Andrew accepted one, as Antonio sometimes took one of his light cigarettes. The swap was no joy to either, merely a courteous ceremony performed while they compared crops.

'Is it a good harvest this year, Antonio?'

'Normal. Not good. Not bad.'

'And the oranges?'

'There's no profit in them. They only want them for juice and that doesn't pay. Olives are better.'

Immediately they were on to the weather again. Antonio craved rain, like everyone else in drought stricken southern Spain. When might it come? Antonio would cast his countryman's eye at the sky and tell us there was no hope of change until the new moon or full moon, whichever was due next. And he was right every time, his weather lore entirely reliable. New weather came with the phases of the moon. Change yes, but not rain. Oh, a trickle here and a shower there, but never the sustained rainfall that was needed and that had once been reliable.

When conversation foundered for lack of a word Antonio asked: 'Do you speak German, Andrés?'

41

Antonio had been sixteen years in a German factory, one of more than a million Spanish men who had become emigrant labourers in the sixties and seventies. In the Alpujarra, the women worked the farms while the men sent money home.

We loaned Antonio the unnamed machine we were using, another offer he may have accepted out of politeness because there was no doubt he preferred sitting on the ground. But we did genuinely need to borrow his *criba* in return, to sort olives from twigs and leaves. The *criba* is a trough of parallel metal rods on four legs, two long legs at the front and shorter ones at the rear. Olives poured in a hopper at the higher end run down into a sack. In theory the leaves and twigs fall between the rods, so you end up with a sack of olives and a pile of debris on the ground. Not so. Much hand work is involved too. Small olives shoot through the grid while twists of leaves and twigs scoot into the sack.

Unwary foreigners' olives weigh less than those picked by locals. We had been warned about this so it was an avoidable mistake that Andrew took our first load to the mill on his own. At the time, it seemed sensible as Patrick and Barbara had to get home before dark to feed their goats, chickens and horses.

'It's all right, I can read a scale and I'll check,' said Andrew, as they loaded the two sacks into the back of our jeep. Our partners used these sacks every year, they estimated we had 100 kilos. Later Andrew admitted, 'It was so dark and the scale was old fashioned, one of those where you move weights up and down rails. I couldn't see properly. And I didn't have my glasses.' He had been handed a chit for 89 kilos.

We learned then that the big sack always weighed in at 79 kilos, the other, half full on Andrew's trip, rather less. Barbara accompanied us on the next delivery and lo! the big sack weighed its normal 79 kilos. However, the millers disparaged olives picked by foreigners. The old man in the flat cap grumbled that ours were too green, too small, in every way not good enough. But his colleagues upended the sacks over a huge hopper and our fruit mingled with everybody else's, all of it looking dismally small and tinged with green.

It was not, locally, a good year for olives and the Alpujarra is not a region that produces juicy ones suitable for preserving. The usual crop is rough stuff to be crushed for oil. Fruit needs to be ripe but not totally black. Neither does the mill welcome big fat olives because after a point the extra weight means they are plump with water.

Word goes round among the farmers when a mill owner has decided the local crop is ready to be harvested. The thrum of mill machinery starts up and the pungent smell of olive oil drifts through the valleys. You either like that smell or you hate it. Fortunately we enjoyed it. Another mill, the only one in the area to offer cold pressing, was planning to open for the season in a few weeks' time and we decided to wait for it. The miller who had insulted us and our olives had been unfair but not absolutely wrong. Our fruit would benefit from longer on the trees.

Andrew used the time to create a vegetable patch on the piece of ground we had earmarked on our first morning. The lower terrace was divided from the rest of our property by huge olive trees at the top of a bank. Neglected vines straggled up through the trees. He hacked back an overgrown pomegranate and cleared weeds using an *azadon*, a mattock, the principal tool of agricultural life in the Alpujarra. At first he tried a spade but could not drive it into the dry soil. The *azadon*, refined over centuries, is the perfect tool. You can swing it like a pick to cut into the ground; use the back to push soil into a ridge; or draw it towards you, using a corner of the blade to make a shallow depression for sowing seeds.

Little could be planted until after the last frost, but Andrew punched holes in the soil and dropped in cloves of garlic. He also untangled and pruned the vines, and supported them on canes to help them grow laterally like a curtain across the bank. Later, when the grapes had grown to full size and ripened, they would be well within our reach.

We planned. Peppers, beans, courgettes, lettuce and herbs would grow well. Lesley added a plea for flowers which could later be transplanted to beds near the house. We were a link in the chain of people who had cared for those acres in much the same way for a thousand years. For us it was especially temporary, an experience to be enjoyed for the sake of experience. Within months we would be returning to London to immerse ourselves in city life. We were not condemned to a life sentence of peasant toil. Just for a short time, we could live in an olive grove . . .

. . . and learn some Spanish. Andrew's teacher was Carmen, a slim, brown-eyed woman in her twenties, who taught at a school in Granada but at weekends visited her boyfriend and gave lessons locally. She brought with her the attitudes of modern Spain, of liberated, well educated women, of environmental concern and freedom from the social strictures of the past. It was, she told Andrew, important that he learn about the real Spanish society as well as the language. They took to discussing reports in *El País*, especially topics that interested her such as the survey which showed that 56 per cent of university places were filled by women and they were working harder and getting better degrees than men.

The day we resumed the olive harvest we worked hard and long. It was dark when we made our first visit to the cold pressing mill in the village of Bayacas. In the gloom the miller's daughter, dressed in trendy blue denim overalls and wellington boots, was shovelling fruit from a mound of olives. Her mother was lifting the buckets and feeding the olives to the mill. Three conical stones revolved on a stone table, crushing flesh and kernels. The clank of a slow engine turning the overhead drive shaft was audible through a wall. Apart from the motor, which had replaced the mule, the method of milling had remained unchanged over hundreds of years.

The miller was taking thick dark paste from the mill and building it into an oozing multi-deck sandwich in the press: first a round esparto grass mat, then a layer of paste, followed by another mat and so on. The smell was richly concentrated, a heavy dark earthy smell, the olfactory equivalent of olive green compared to other shades of green.

Mother and daughter broke off to deal with our load. The daughter went outside and reappeared at a window high on the wall above the weighing machine. She dangled an electric light bulb, no more

45

powerful than a candle. Dark eyes caught the gleam as she leaned through the whitewashed aperture. We were going to describe it as a Caravaggio effect, until we remembered the painter preferred boys. By this soft glow we were invited to read the scales.

We received oil in part payment – cloudy, viscid green oil – and a chit for the balance to be paid later in cash. The flavour was stronger than any oil we had tasted before, although we were used to buying rich green Greek oil in London. Our oil had a special taste but did not overpower. It never cleared completely, although our experiments proved that standing bottles in sunlight speeded the process.

Most of the oil pressed in the Alpujarra is consumed there. What the growers do not take in payment is sold locally. Any surplus goes to the big-scale producers in the neighbouring province of Jaen. There the millions of compact trees, set in rows and harvested by machine, give the countryside the appearance of an enormous embroidery decorated with French knots. Some of the oil from here reaches Britain via bottling plants in Italy.

Not all of our crop went to the mill. Lesley was inordinately proud of the fruit she cured herself. Olives are inedible until cured, a lengthy process. She chose some that were beginning to ripen, part green, part mahogany; then slit them with a knife, washed them and placed them in a plastic bucket. She covered them with water, changing it every day for a month until the olives no longer tasted bitter. Next they were transferred to brine made with three table-spoons of salt for each pint of water. Cloves of garlic were added along with quartered lemons, sprigs of thyme and crushed coriander seeds.

After two weeks in brine the olives were ready to eat or to be bottled with more lemon juice, garlic and coriander and covered with oil. Although recipe books suggested bottling in brine, as the Spanish do unless they prefer vinegar, Lesley liked to use our own olive oil. It enhanced the flavour and prevented mould forming on the surface.

Our home cured olives were an astonishing success. Everyone who sampled them wanted the recipe, once they accepted we had not found a special shop to supply us. Ours were subtly different to the ones prepared commercially nearby. For this we thanked Chris, the Greek Cypriot who had a shop in London's Chapel Market. He had taught us how to flavour them with coriander. Chris sold green ones already cracked for this purpose, but any green olives can be flavoured. Purists argue that they should be cracked by bashing them, but that is messy and a nick with a knife works equally well. The recipe is simple: bottle the fruit in oil with lemon juice, garlic and coriander, and leave for one week before enjoying.

Our Alpujarran olive harvest was a lengthy affair because we paused to allow the fruit to ripen further, we gardened, made sightseeing trips, and we had visitors to stay. Also it was backbreaking and we were under no pressure to do it every day. For our neighbours it was different. Day after day, Maria, her husband and sister-in-law rattled among their trees, used a broom on their bare earth, and scrabbled on hands and knees to the accompaniment of his sad song. Friends and neighbours joined them.

One of the bits of information tossed to us by our stream of callers was that olives that fell on to our land from neighbours' trees did not become ours and we must avoid picking them up. Once the harvest began, we grew used to finding unfamiliar men and women helping Maria or Antonio track down their strays, on the edge of our patio and on our roof, but there was still a surprise. One day Lesley was writing, deep in silence, when there was a frightening rumbling as though the roof was caving in. She shot outside and ran up to the roof terrace, to find Maria's friends running one of those nameless machines up and down and spiking their olives.

At weekends voices rose in laughter and happy conversation from *cortijos* along the *camino*. Men like Antonio, who worked these toy farms during the week, were joined by their families who had come to share in the harvest. No one was too young or too old to snatch runaway olives from the ground; to trim *caña* from the supply that, handily, grew on odd corners of land all around; or to weigh fruit in his hand and say that crops these days were not as good as they used to be.

CHAPTER SIX

FIREWORKS
FOR A SAINT

APART FROM THE OLIVE HARVEST, there is little to be done on a fruit farm in winter. Very few of our orange trees were ripe, although we had enough for juice and jellies. While sharp, they made excellent marmalade, in place of the bitter Seville orange, but we did not bother to make our own. Friends who begged oranges for marmalade-making kept us supplied with jars from their kitchens. Our lemon curd became popular though.

It was going to be months before we had to consider harvesting the oranges, and there were too few lemon trees for us to sell any of the fruit. Almonds and other fruit trees were wintering. It allowed us time to look around. For one thing, we wanted to investigate the building that stands at the highest point of Órgiva. It is a striking white octagon with a red tiled roof, and we wondered about it every time we approached the town. But once we were in the town, it disappeared. As we seemed unlikely to stumble upon it by chance, we set out to find it.

Away from the shops of the square and main street, the hill rose more steeply, up through cobbled alleyways where black iron balconies trailed pink geraniums and caged birds sang. Front doors opened into low dark rooms. We could have been in any Alpujarran village, except that we saw no animals on the ground floors. Then we came to a tilted square and there it was, the white octagon that looks like the mosque it once was but which is now the chapel of St Sebastian. No signs had pointed our way and hardly anyone visited it. We knew people who had lived in or close to the town for years without ever going there. The uphill trudge deterred them, but the panorama made it worth the effort. We squinted through a spyhole in the door. The chapel, as so often with Andalusian churches, was locked.

Another time Andrew returned with a friend and they were luckier. On the steps sat a girl aged about twelve who saved them squinting by producing the key. Inside, the chapel is a tranquil white space. The polychrome figure of the martyr faces the door, with saints in niches flanking him like bodyguards.

Hardly was Christmas over than the evenings were full of the whizzes and bangs of fireworks as the devil was scared away from parading saints. We seemed to be under attack: fusillades opened up from one village to be answered by another and then another. From our roof we watched as Órgiva and two nearby villages

celebrated St Sebastian's day, January 20. Two other
villages had been loud in praise of St Anthony three
days earlier. Mountains rolled the sound around and
flung it back with a deep rumbling.

We went into Órgiva to watch *Estaban*, the procession of the figure of St Sebastian from the church
in the square to his chapel up the hill. A volley of
Chinese crackers announced his emergence from the
church with a noise that was painful, even with hands
over ears. People had been herded back, an acknowl-
edgement that the practice is dangerous in other ways
too. A couple of years earlier a shop window had
been blown out and a man lost a leg.

With the sound reverberating in the mountains, the
statues moved off from the church steps, to begin a
slow journey marked with ambushes of rockets, the
noisy whoosh and bang type.

'I feel tall,' said Lesley. At five foot four she had a
clear view over most of the crowd. Without meaning
to, we joined the procession. This was difficult to
avoid because the streets were too narrow to accom-
modate spectators, apart from those looking down
between the potted plants of their balconies. We
snaked along for what seemed miles, a halting progress as the men carrying the saint and the Virgin
jiggled the heavy flower-decked thrones around tight
corners. From time to time they set them down while
their aching limbs revived. Women outnumbered men
in the procession, although there was a fair mix of old
and young, of family groups and individuals.

In the upper town there is a leafy square with old
houses along one side and blocks of modern flats
facing. We were greeted by another deafening fusil-

51

lade organized by the teams of professionals hired to set off the fireworks. No one else appeared to enjoy this degree of noise, it was something endured rather as some women were enduring the walk in stockinged feet. Out went the street lights, and lamps on the Virgin's throne fell off. An icy wind whipped across the open space. The pauses were stretching as the bearers needed increasingly long periods for recuperation. Fortunately we had the band to cheer us, playing the same tune over and over, a catchy hymn although no one sang. Throughout, the procession was quiet, not straining to be silent but murmuring conversation, greeting friends along the way, and relighting guttering candles.

At last we reached the octagonal chapel, greeted with yet more appalling noise, but then the real fireworks started: cascading spangles and stars, beautiful and elaborate fireworks that flew up over our heads and painted pictures in the night sky directly above us. The crowd came to life, Ooohing and Aaahing, loving it, loving the way it went on and on, extravagantly. It was as though their column had been an army fighting its way up through the town under attack from hostile forces and now it had won the hill and was celebrating. They loved it. But it was the last time we were to see more than a couple of pretty fireworks at any festival in the Alpujarra.

When the last sparks of colour faded, the chapel bell tolled its flat, cracked sound as a pair of boys in the tower took turns to swing it by hand, over and over, eagerly, unevenly. And while this was going on the statues were carried towards the building. Women reached out to St Sebastian and plucked flowers from his throne, red carnations for the martyr's blood, white ones for purity. He went inside a bit ragged. People surged after him and helped themselves too so that when we wandered back down through the streets moonlight played on the red and the white in their hands.

Home after midnight, the pierced wall light on the patio guided our last steps. We paused to look down at the curving wall of the dining-room with its stained-glass window, at the shadows of leaves on the white walls, at the faintly glowing oranges. Seeing the house in this gentle light always made us think how lucky we were to have this piece of paradise for a while. Beauty swept all doubts from the mind. The lamp was soft as candlelight, hiding imperfections.

On the patio we discovered we were not alone. This time the visitor was a warty toad, the biggest we had ever seen. Andrew, wanting to protect it from the cats, carried it into the grass near the pond. Twenty minutes later it was back, creeping past the kitchen door. Apparently our patio was a customary path for migrating toads as well as people. The cats took no interest in this creature, which we later identified as a Spanish spadefoot. They had other things on their minds. Sex, for instance. Cosmo was less than a year old and, we had been told, there was plenty of time for her owner to have her spayed. Posy had already been done. Alas, no one had explained to the ginger cat from Maria's *cortijo* and he was being a nuisance.

Cosmo was a shy cat, a tabby with black patches and stripes on fur that felt like a silk rug. She had the small head and streamlined body of the African cat, amber eyes and nose, and ear tufts. She was elegant.

Being young, she liked to play but Posy would not. Posy preferred to snooze on a chair and make occasional dashes up olive trees, she liked to hog the food bowl and push Cosmo out. It was because of Posy that we had been left that array of expensive cat food. When it was used up we switched to Spanish cheapomix. Posy made a disdainful exit. She lay on her chair, giving us the coldest of her cold looks. She was rather good at those. But she missed only one meal.

With the unwelcome attentions of Ginger the cats were both on tenterhooks day and night, and needed a chaperone while they ate. We fretted when Cosmo failed to appear at mealtimes – not because she might go hungry, she was a skilful hunter – but afraid she might be deterred from staying at the house.

She grew perverse, spitting at Ginger when he was near, answering his wailing call when he was away on the terraces, and racing to us for sanctuary when he came back again. Too much of the action took place on the long L-shaped patio. It was tiring and tiresome for everyone. We had kept the cats outside, but Lesley was weakening, arguing that Cosmo had nowhere to hide. Andrew was sterner, refusing to have the house turned into a refuge for battered she cats. He caught her discussing the position with Cosmo.

'If you're rape counselling a cat, forget it,' he said. 'It's nature.'

But nature kept him awake too. There was the nightingale that disturbed us every night, singing from the orange tree near our window. Wonderful once in a while, but not every night. And now when the bird was not performing, the cats were. As the house rested against a bank, Ginger took to chasing our pair the length of the roof, down the steps by our bedroom window, along the patio, up the woodpile, back on to the roof and . . . round and round and round. This, and the accompanying shrieks, seemed to go on all night long.

We retaliated during the day, shooing Ginger fiercely, but he was too fast. We chased him away down one end of the patio and he was over the terraces, right round and approaching from the other direction before we could get our breath back.

'What does Maria feed him on? Steroids?'

But there was no answer because the other one of us was chasing him off again.

Then one morning Lesley, who was on chaperone duty while Cosmo ate, scared him away in the direction of our bedroom and, as she turned back, spotted him already on the woodpile. But no, he was slinking away towards the washing line. Two of them!

'This isn't nature, it's gang rape,' she said. Cosmo was a nervous wreck, eating and peeing poised for flight, changed from a shy but affectionate cat into a wretched one. Suddenly it stopped. When either of the Gingers came by it was only to steal food.

We had never had kittens before. Puppies yes, but not kittens. We drew up a mental list of pet lovers who could advise us what, if anything, we ought to do. Very little, we imagined, as Cosmo was not a pedigree cat nor a soft-living pet. She was a *campo* cat, a country cat, who lived and roamed and hunted out in the open.

'She'll go off one day and have her kittens out in the *campo*, and she'll bring them home to you when she's ready,' said Judit, the Dutch plumber whose own *campo* cat did that.

Judit had dropped in to investigate damp in the wall between the kitchen and a spare bedroom. The problem was apparently in pipes near the stopcock and meter, but this run of pipework was encased, not in the Spanish way behind plaster but in concrete which had to be chipped off. She simplified the pipework, repaired the leak and fixed the meter as it should be, in an outside cupboard where the meter reader could gain access to it.

With one leak repaired, we switched our attention to another. The swimming pool leaked. And as everyone kept warning us, it was essential to fix it because in Andalusia in summer a pool was not a luxury.

CHAPTER SEVEN

THE UGLY,
THE DRY
AND THE DIRTY

'Year of snow, year of wealth,' said Rafael. He looked through the window of our car, up towards the mountains, and frowned. There was a thin mantle of snow, not sufficient to melt slowly, filter through the ground and water the land for the rest of the year. He saw no hope of a year of wealth.

The Alpujarra was enduring the third relatively dry winter in a row. Rafael was worried. Like everyone else he talked about water. It had always been a local preoccupation, but after several almost rainless winters, coupled with gloomy forecasts about changing weather patterns in Africa and Europe, there was a well-founded fear that the water would run out. The planned reservoir, if it went ahead, would serve the coastal towns and farms. A dam would be built across the Guadalfeo a few miles below Órgiva, and the reservoir would be three and a half miles long, big enough to offer hope of less aridity in the valley. But the people of the Alpujarra were sceptical. Andalusian reservoirs had been below their optimum levels for years, how would one in the Guadalfeo be filled? Only by cutting back on the amount of water that ran through the *acequias*, the irrigation channels. Rafael doubted the dam would ever be built.

We first met Rafael by giving him a lift into town. Buses were scarce and hitching lifts common. A wiry man with a limp, he proved a non-stop chatterer. Naturally, his conversation with us opened with a series of questions about our means and our children. His trips to town were frequent because it was there he met his friends, for more talk.

As we let him out of the car in the square that first day and shook hands, he swore his unending thanks. Whenever we saw him on the road after that we gave him a lift, and each time he thanked us with the same lavish courtesy.

For a few years he had worked in a factory in Barcelona, which was where he had had an accident. This brought him a pension and a reason to return to his beloved Alpujarra. His own father, like Antonio, had spent many years working in Germany. When he returned, Rafael and his brother and three sisters were grown up. Until then, they had seen their father for only a few weeks each summer.

Rafael grew vegetables to supplement his pension but his days were mainly spent in talk. Like all Spaniards he wanted others to share his love of his birthplace. He was happy living in his village, far happier than he had ever been in Catalonia. He regarded his limp as a piece of luck that had brought him home. It was with the same philosophical acceptance that he anticipated the drying up and changing of the landscape that was so dear to him. 'When God wishes he makes sun and rain,' he said. He often dropped these old sayings into conversation. In Spanish they rhymed.

For us, one of the oddest sights in Spain was the dry river. A contradiction in terms, surely. River beds might be wide, the channels deep, but in them there would be nothing but grey dust and boulders. Or they might be steep gullies floored with shingle. Or they might be clear of stones and used for driving along instead of man-made roads.

Near Órgiva are four rivers but only the Guadalfeo, curiously named the ugly river, flows all year. The others are the Seco, literally the dry river; the Sucio, the dirty river because its water is stained by ore; and the Chico, the boy, a name for which no one offered us an explanation. The Guadalfeo is one of the major rivers of Andalusia and it approaches the coast through a magnificent gorge. But it is dry long before then, the last of its water taken for a seaside town. Once, after heavy storms, we saw it bubbling through the gorge and on through the channel that carries it across the coastal plain to the sea. We were astonished that it remembered the way!

Great bridges span these dry rivers, a precaution against torrents that sweep away roads, houses and whole villages. Several years before we moved into our olive grove, there had been a winter of torrential rain. The disaster started with a storm one night. After that it rained for about six weeks. *Cortijos* were cut off, by floodwater or because mountainsides had slipped across roadways and mule tracks.

Even when there was no physical damage to complain of, it was a very uncomfortable period to live through. *Launa* roofs leaked. Woodpiles were saturated so that fires were smoky. Brown mould colonized walls. Washing would not dry in front of sluggish fires. Shopping was impossible. Food stocks ran out. Stepping outside, to fetch drinking water from the spring or tend animals, meant getting drenched.

Friends who had survived that dreadful winter told tales of ingenuity and endurance. To have shared in those unnerving events was to be a part of the social history of the area, to have earned a place in folklore. One of the questions new acquaintances always asked us was: 'Were you here *that* winter?' We had to admit we were not members of the survivors' club, but we did enjoy their tales. We also enjoyed the way the stories were gathering details in the telling, nourishment for a growing myth. Yet it had not been pure heroics, with figures staggering along slippery tracks in blinding rain to beat on doors in distant villages and beg food for babies. We also knew people who could not bear it and tried to leave, only to discover they were stuck. Where there had been a road, there was only a river.

Although the rivers are normally dry, or virtually so, one of the constantly delightful things about the Alpujarra is the sound of running water. It gushes and gurgles along the *acequias*, it flashes whitely down hillsides and races beside roads. On a hot day someone on a distant patch of land will switch an irrigation channel, and suddenly your afternoon is enriched by the music of water.

These intermittent streams can be perplexing. Friends of ours were astonished to spot a baby waterfall near the cottage where they were on holiday; and even more astonished when an hour or so later there was no trace of it.

'An *acequia*,' we said, and had to explain because they knew nothing about the irrigation system.

'When can we have our waterfall back?'

'Probably the same time next week, depending on the land owner's water rights.'

Faces fell. They were going home in two days. They never saw their waterfall again.

Each holding has its jealously guarded water rights. Our olive grove was irrigated weekly, on Thursdays. The water arrived with a whoosh at mid-day and then, for precisely an hour and a half, we had the use of a cool mountain stream. We were lucky. Some people got their water in the middle of the night and had to work by torch light.

Valley and mountainside are criss-crossed by channels, with metal gates at junctions to divert the flow from one *huerta*, or piece of irrigated land, to another. Junctions can be anywhere: in gullies, alongside fields, beside roads or under *caminos*. Sometimes they are in the centre of *caminos* and as often as not the stones which should cover them are missing.

We knew the danger points leading to our olive grove, three places where the car must be wiggled to straddle gaps, but unfamiliar *caminos* were a risk. One day, having negotiated a gaping junction, we found our way blocked by a parked car. The owner was working in a field. He came over but not, as we assumed, to move his car. Although there was a driveway he could have pulled into he refused, saying it was too steep. Instead, he urged Andrew to reverse beyond the junction and drive up again on the other side of it so the angle of approach to the parked car was marginally more favourable. This was ridiculous, especially as our spare wheel partly blocked our rear view. With limited Spanish it was difficult to explain and hopeless to argue. The man continued to offer arm-waving advice. Andrew, though, had ideas of his own. With the memorable reassurance, 'It's all right, I know what I'm doing,' he reversed down the hole.

We had never needed our four wheel drive before. It was useless. The vehicle rested on its axle, the rear wheel dangling in space. Unless that wheel could grip on something, we could not drive out. We tried wedges of wood, all the usual tricks. None worked. A silent man and a grey mule with panniers of plaited grass came to watch. The man scratched his chin and stared, but the mule lost interest and browsed along the bank. Men were fetched from farms and fields. They lifted the jeep and shoved it back on to the track. That particular junction did not gape again, in future a large stone protected it.

The junction where we switched water to our land was uncovered but as it was at the end of the mule track there was no danger to traffic. During winter, when water was plentiful because fewer people were using it, we flood irrigated, letting it rush and gush across the olive grove until the trees seemed to float on a swamp. In summer, when there was less, runnels were cut with an *azadon* to direct the flow so that it nurtured individual trees.

To water the vegetable patch on the lower land we sent the stream coursing down the slope by the washing line. When green shoots of garlic were pushing up, Andrew decided it was time to sow his seeds: peppers, beans and lettuce, also marguerites, because Lesley loves every kind of daisy.

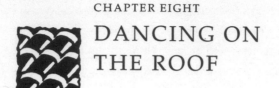

CHAPTER EIGHT

DANCING ON
THE ROOF

MANY OF THE SCENES we saw daily were biblical. A man bent beneath a load of fodder climbed a slender path; or a woman drove a goat along a cobbled alley. It looked as though it had gone on for ever and would go on for ever.

But we were watching the last generation of subsistence farmers. Too many people had fled the land for flats and factory jobs in Barcelona or Madrid for it to be otherwise. Village populations had halved in thirty years. Life on the land was as tough as ever, it was not going to make these small farmers a part of Spain's economic miracle. Cinema and television had shown them a different way.

The ending of peasant farming, with the consequent collapse of terraces and *acequias*, threatens an environmental disaster. Already land is scorched and trees are dying for lack of attention and water. Goats, rain and wind cut channels of erosion through the dry earth. Terraces which only twenty years ago were green with watered crops now pass through the seasons in the drab brown that is the colour of neglect. The Spanish government is seeking ways of keeping the Alpujarra green. Greenness brings tourists and tourism has become the region's second largest money-maker, second only to the curing of hams. Reafforestation is high among the priorities because trees look good and slow the run-off of rain allowing it to soak into the ground.

Although the peasant life has been hard, the Alpujarra is not a place where people starved. The diet was restricted but nourishing; largely vegetarian, but supplemented by fish and occasional meat. Day labourers who worked on the huge farms in other parts of Andalusia were the ones who had suffered. Centuries of discontent with the *latifundia*, as the system of large farms and absentee landlords was called, lay at the root of many of Spain's political upheavals.

By contrast, the *minifundia* of the Alpujarra saved people from the worst hunger. Even in the bad times, when crops failed, there had been what Rafael said they used to call the stew pot of half starvation – much cabbage and little meat.

Time and again, stories of life in the Alpujarra came back to the wonder of those *acequias*, begun by the Romans and developed by the Moors in their 700 year reign. After the Kingdom of Granada fell to the Catholic Kings in 1492, the Moors were allowed to keep the Alpujarra. Their final expulsion was delayed until 1570, after uprisings and bloody retributions. More than 96,000 people went. In each village a couple of Moorish families, converted to Christianity and called Moriscos, were obliged to remain to work the irrigation system and, in many instances, to care for the mulberry trees that sustained the important silk industry. Nearly 2,500 families from Leon, Galicia, Asturias and Castile were brought in to repopulate the area.

Over the following centuries, the population rose and fell and crops changed, but the irrigation system always survived. Andrew traced the sources of *acequias* in crystal mountain streams where trout shimmered in pools beneath cascades of water and greenery. It was wonderful walking country but we had to rely on people suggesting routes to us as there were no handy plans to follow. Towards the end of our stay a Spanish publisher produced a book of walks.

Andrew did several of his walks with Mike Lelliot who had advertised walking holidays and then realized he had to invent the walks before his guests arrived. Together he and Andrew pored over maps. They often chose to follow *acequias*. The engineering achievement was a marvel. For miles the channels hugged the mountainsides, plunging into tunnels to cross from one valley to another, or streaming from a high level to a lower one. They led deep into extraordinarily beautiful country and often provided the only access to it.

Mike planned to take his holidaymakers up high enough to appreciate the most spectacular view points. On one favourite walk he and Andrew climbed in shirtsleeves through snow, to emerge on the ridge between the Chico and Poqueira valleys. All around lay abandoned fields where, until recently, rye grew. It was easy to picture a reaper straightening his back beneath the sun and wasting a moment to consider the Mediterranean spread out below and the dark outline of the Rif mountains of Morocco.

Rye became a widespread crop after the Moors left, one of the numerous changes the repopulators made. Once we had learned how many things they changed, we became intrigued that they bothered to retain the Moorish vernacular architecture. We used to play a trick on our friends around Órgiva, showing them a photograph Andrew took ten years before of a Berber village in the Anti-Atlas mountains of Morocco, and asking whether they recognized it. Usually they thought they did. Some decided it was in the eastern Alpujarra. Others identified it as one of the nearer villages, taken before it was painted white. No one guessed that it wasn't even in Spain! The white painted mosque looked, at first sight, like a church. The line of *chumba*, prickly pear cactus, in the foreground of the picture was characteristic too. *Chumba*, growing in dry land, makes goat-proof hedges, provides sweet fruit, and is a durable wind-break for Alpujarran and Moroccan villages. We intended to pick some when the waxy yellow flowers had died away and the fruit ripened, but we never had gloves with us. We had done it many years before without protection and found their hair-like spines painful and almost impossible to remove from our skin: not something we would suffer again.

The clue that our photograph was not taken locally

was obvious, once it had been pointed out. 'I knew there was something. There are no chimneys,' a friend said after we had revealed the truth. The chimneys are a motif of the region, on postcards and covers of guide books. The stacks rise three or four feet from the roofs and are topped by flat stones on four legs. The exact design varies from village to village: in some they are cylinders and in others rectangular. Some villages favour cementing a smaller stone on top of the capping stone, while others prefer to shape the top of the chimney with plaster to resemble a cardinal's broad-brimmed berettino.

To an extent, available materials dictated that stone houses of the Alpujarra continued to be built in the Moorish way. The characteristic flat roofs are covered with *launa*, a grey shale of decomposing rock which slides together when wet to form an impermeable layer. In other words, mud. The layer of *launa* is spread on large flat stones which in turn rest on wooden beams. But that is in the higher villages. Lower down, where *caña* grows, closely packed canes replace the stones. The result is a flexible building, capable of withstanding the tremors of this earthquake region. These days it is normal to incorporate a plastic sheet between the *launa* and the rest because *launa* roofs are not rain proof. Hot sun dries mud and cracks it, so these roofs leak.

It was late afternoon when ours began to leak. A lashing wind had whipped clouds down the valley and the sky darkened. Briefly, rain tipped down. The fig tree was rattling its bare branches against our windows as though begging to be let in. Nature was being noisy. But suddenly a separate sound began, that unmistakable tap, tap, tap of water hitting a hard floor. The ceiling of one of our spare bedrooms was leaking.

Lesley pulled on her wellies and seized an umbrella. 'I'll go. I've always wanted to do this.'

'But it's pouring.'

'I think you *have* to do it in the rain.'

She ran up the outside steps, calculated when she was above the drip and shuffled the launa about with her boot. There was a dip there, a puddle. She smoothed away the dip and sent a stream of grey and gritty water over the side of the roof. Then she stamped around, compressing the *launa*.

All this she had learned from Gerald Brenan's *South from Granada*, where he had written that during a rainstorm in Yegen each house had somebody dancing about on the roof. Now she realized his delightful description lacked an essential detail – he had not mentioned how long you needed to go on with it. She stamped a bit more. Wind whistled round and flung the run off from her umbrella down her neck. She decided she had probably stamped enough and went indoors to check. The ceiling no longer dripped.

Although rain was rare, what we got usually came through the roof. Ours had been laid by an Englishman who had not grasped the principals involved and had not sieved the *launa*. Unsieved it was less able to form an impermeable layer. We had leaks that trickled down walls and left grey streaks, leaks in several ceilings including the one where Maria's friends had run the spiked olive-collecting machine, and a leak that sent water splashing through the light socket in the bathroom. We ran on the roof and fixed them.

But the most persistent leak was in the wardrobe in our bedroom and there was nothing we could do about that one. It was beneath our paved roof terrace. *Launa* proved far easier to deal with.

We had yet to deal with the swimming pool which leaked inwards every time we irrigated, forming a puddle of brackish water at the bottom. It was a job for an expert and that is how we met Josef, known as German José.

CHAPTER NINE

FIESTA!

'I CAN'T WORK HERE. There are too many interruptions. Do you realize seven people called today?' Lesley said one evening. As it was a sunny day, she had taken her typewriter to the patio to work on her new novel. 'It's worse than London. There I have a front door, here I can't pretend I'm not home.'

One of the seven was German José. A tall slim man with close-cropped hair, he danced down the track like a frenetic member of a modern dance company. José went everywhere at speed, gabbling his broken English.

'I come. I mend pool.'

'Oh, er, good.'

He surveyed the route a lorry might take across the abandoned land to bring in materials. There followed some of that building trade head-shaking.

'Not good access here.'

Rapidly he explained how he was going to line the pool and then he rushed away. Someone, unkindly, had nicknamed him Manic José because of the sheer speed with which he attacked everything.

At least, Lesley admitted that evening, he was a useful visitor, he had come to do something for us. Her other interrupters had been a goatherd filling his water bottle; two Grundies asking whether Sally had left anything for them; a friend who wanted to show someone our peculiar bathroom; and a back-packer on his way to a camp across the river. It was an average sort of day.

'It's unbelievable,' Lesley said, 'but this is the least private place I've ever lived in.'

Cries of *'Hola! Hola!'* drowned Andrew's reply. The next wave of visitors was upon us. He found three smartly dressed men. They called him *hombre*, patted him on the shoulder and looked around our lighted terrace exclaiming *bonita*, pretty. Then they got down to business. They wanted a donation towards the costs of the fiesta of *Cristo de la Expiración* when Órgiva's famous statue of Christ on the Cross is paraded. We had been tipped off they would seek us out. 'You can't give a couple of hundred pesetas,' advised one of our mentors. 'It has to be at least the price of a three-course meal.'

So Andrew borrowed a pen and wrote his name and the price of a three-course meal on the collection sheet. In return he was given tickets for a raffle although we were ambivalent about winning a picture of the statue. More handshakes, pats on the back and affectionate *hombres* and they were gone.

'Collecting for fireworks,' Andrew explained, back at the fireside.

'What's the fiesta?'

Opening a guide book he gave a halting translation. ' "The Thursday before *Dolores* . . ." '

'When is that?'

'A couple of weeks before Easter.'

He read on. ' ". . . takes place the festival of Cristo de la Expiración. The most significant moment is the procession lasting until dawn with the image of Christ during which is produced an unusual and noisy waste" . . . no, I think it means "extravagance" here . . . "of fireworks, crackers and rockets, without equal in the region." '

'I wish we could stipulate our fiver is spent on the pretty ones.'

We froze at new cries of '*Hola!*' More visitors. But no, the collecting team had returned, begging the pen Andrew had forgotten to give back.

Before the fiesta Cosmo gave birth. We had discovered her exploring a dark space beneath a bed but friends who knew about these matters were adamant that as she was a *campo* cat she would choose open country for the birth. As she had not heard this theory, Cosmo had her kittens in one of our tea chests. A few weeks earlier we had put it on the patio, with an old rug in it, just in case. After nose-wrinkling consideration, she had taken a few naps there.

One night we woke to the sound of trees buffeted by gales and raindrops flung against our window. Morning was calmer but dark and drear. Going on to the patio we missed the usual clamour from cats demanding breakfast. Posy was coiled on her chair.

We peered into the tea chest and Cosmo stared back with her golden-eyed gaze. Then something moved, as if one of the dark patches in the design of her fur had begun to creep. She bent her head to it and gave a soft purr.

With the coming of the kittens, she acquired new language. She had been a cat who seldom purred but expressed her delight in squeakier ways. Motherhood provided her with a full repertoire of purrs and growls, hisses and murmurs; of warnings, admonishments and encouragements. While she was feeding the kittens we gave her milk which she would come and ask for, but not with her typical squeaks. The sound she used was so much like 'meeelk' that it made the hairs rise on the back of one's neck.

There were five kittens. The biggest was black with white feet, a pushy puss who was first to do everything including voyaging out of the tea chest. We called him Columbus. Then there was a tortoiseshell, a pretty mix of white and black and ginger. As she was implicated in most of Columbus's adventures she became Isabella. The rest were tabbies, later to show flecks of ginger but at the beginning like diminutive Cosmos. We lumped them together as the Look-alikes.

More visitors drifted through, making detours to drool over the kittens. José began and ended each session on the pool by booming German endearments into the tea chest. Carmen, Andrew's Spanish teacher, rounded off each lesson with five minutes cooing. Everybody loved them.

Everybody loved them but nobody wanted them. There were too many kittens around. *'Es primavera,'* sighed Elena, who had dropped in, the way people did. Her husband was working with José. 'All the kittens come in the spring.' A design fault in the making of the world then, no reflection on our kittens.

'How do *you* cope?' Lesley asked Sue, who owned Cosmo's mother and each spring found homes for a litter.

Sue said it was not too difficult because she offered good hunters. 'We keep them until they are three months old because the mother cat doesn't teach them to hunt until the third month.'

We had supposed that skills were innate, not taught. One of the fascinating things, when the kittens were very new and more like smudges of fluff than specific animals, was the way they would attempt cattish gestures. A limb would waver towards a head and a paw would practise grooming. Somehow they knew they were going to be cats. But now we were learning that their development was not entirely instinctive. Cosmo was a good hunter, so we decided to keep her kittens until she had taught them.

Soon it was fiesta time. We went into town and took up position but not without trepidation. In the plaza were metal stands with crackers strung between them. Racks of rockets were lined up. Police were moving the crowd back, but we kept our attention on the man who would light the touch paper because one had to be quick to get hands over ears. If you have ever heard a distress signal fired in Britain to call out a lifeboat, you will know what a tremendous volume of sound a rocket produces. Órgiva's way of celebrating was to fire them in salvoes of fifty, salvo after salvo. And between them came the explosive rattle of those strings of crackers.

Once the smoke and the smell of gunpowder had cleared a bit we approached the church. The statue was not being displayed at the door as we had been told it would be, so we went inside. Two men were holding it upright on a table while the devout queued to kiss its leg. Some clutched tissues and reached up as if to wipe sweat from the torso.

During the procession it rained. Undaunted, hundreds of people, some barefoot, set out to follow the statue through the night. In each street it was honoured with a firework display; bangs and flashes, very few pretty flares. In the top square it became stuck for two hours with repeat performances outside each block of flats. Fed up with the weather, the noise and the sulphurous stink, we left them to it.

That was the most important fiesta of Órgiva's year. For other Andalusian towns the highlight was *Semana Santa*, Holy Week, when parades on a grand scale take place. Their saintly statues are accompanied by confraternities in robes of white, purple, brown or other colours, faces hidden beneath conical hoods. Bands and slow marching soldiers set the pace. The big processions are smoothly stage managed, essential in a big town like Granada where several churches will show their treasures simultaneously. Preparations take weeks. The heavy wooden and silver *pasos* on which the statues are carried must be polished. Men train so they are fit to take the crushing weight.

And the statues themselves? One day, in an Alpujarran village church we saw the Virgin Mary, her modesty covered by a freshly laundered cream cotton shift but her hands unscrewed and lying on a shelf. She was like an exquisite shop window mannequin. We did not realize she was Mary, undressed like that there were none of the clues. Three or four people were fussing over her. One fastened a pearl necklace around her throat, others made appreciative grunts as they admired the way the pearls gleamed against her pale painted skin.

'You have a procession soon?' we asked.

A man tweaked the lace of her sleeve to straighten it. 'Yes, we are preparing.'

'Who's the patron of the village?' We assumed this was her figure.

'St George.' With a quick nod of the head he indicated a statue across the church.

'He's the patron saint of England too. April the twenty-fourth, isn't it?'

The man corrected Andrew who always gets dates wrong. 'The twenty-third.'

'So what are you doing now?'

'Getting ready for Easter.'

A woman arrived with a dress held out carefully so as not to crease it. Together they lifted it over Mary's head. We left them then, saving a final glance for the hands lying on the shelf.

The quality of many of the statues is very fine, their fabric clothes exquisite. Others are made entirely of carved wood, the carving and painting marvellously realistic. It seemed a pity for them not to have the wardrobe, if only because dressing up the figures is one of the quieter pleasures of the noisy Andalusian fiestas.

The visitors we were expecting for Easter were keen

to see the parades in Granada. We had qualms about how well Stephen and Claire, our London neighbours, would adapt to our rural home with its beauties and discomforts. To add to its problems the washing machine was being temperamental. Before coming to us they were to stay at a hotel near Málaga reputed to be among the world's best. Anyone might balk at slumping from world class luxury to sharing an eccentric bathroom and sleeping in a damp bedroom with a quota of exotic insects inside and a flurry of kittens to trip over outside.

We need not have worried. The hotel was not all it claimed to be and on the day they left a national strike of waiters began. They had to pour their own orange juice from cartons. At least we could offer fresh juice from tree to glass in seconds. For resting and reading, which is what they craved, our olive grove was perfect.

The best point at which to see an Easter Week procession is when it comes out of the church. We chose the Good Friday procession from the church of Santa Ana in the Plaza Nueva, below the Alhambra hill. Our timing went awry and we were early, so we let the beat of a distant drum lure us to another parade first. This one was full of unintentional comedy. Eyes glinting from slits in pointy hoods of the *penitentes* wore too much mascara. And among the contingent of women in black, solemn and elegant beneath the high combs and lace veils of the *mantilla* head-dress, came a handful wearing spindly shoes and skirts that were shorter than the fall of their veils, young women whose eyes chased over the male faces in the crowd.

Back in the Plaza Nueva another crowd was forming, not outside the church but in front of the nearby Royal Chancellery. A television van was there: *Canal Sur*, the Andalusian television channel, was providing all-day live coverage of the festival in the major cities. The doors opened exactly on time and we saw the *pasos* with figures of Mary and Christ. The base of a *paso* is like a huge chest with curtains hanging to the ground. Behind the curtains are the men who, on a discreet signal, lift the throne and carry it forward. If you look down, you can spot the trainer-shod centipede feet taking their short shuffling steps.

But first through the doors came the *penitentes* covered in robes and pointed hoods. Then Mary slowly emerged, with the rolling, swaying movement that characterizes the progress of a statue on parade. This polychrome figure, hands held to the breast, eyes cast slightly upwards, was exceptionally well carved, every fold of the cream dress and blue cape finely detailed. A halo radiated from her head. She stood on a bed of red flowers before a black and silver cross with angels at its foot and a pure white cloth billowing from the transom. The crowd was silent. Only when she was clear of the building was there an eruption of applause. The *paso* bearing Christ followed, as the Virgin always takes precedence in the Easter Week processions.

The Santa Ana parade had all the dignity of devotion. Yet something threatening happens when men submerge their own identities into that of a confraternity. It looks like an exercise, a demonstration of power, and that is exactly what it used to be. By taking its treasures and its supporters clubs on to the streets, the church reminded everyone where power lay.

Holy Week processions are slow, stopping every

few yards to let the bearers rest. Before the two figures were out of the Plaza Nueva, we had gone in search of food.

We found a table at the Duende, a pleasant restaurant with a menu of Spanish food and posters of bullfighters decorating its walls. *Duende* means imp but also, in the words of the Granada poet Lorca, 'a mysterious power which everyone senses and no philosopher explains'. There was no mystery about what affected the restaurant that evening. Waiters were on strike and family and friends were standing in. Thirsty, we ordered mineral water immediately. Bottles came but the caps stayed on because the stand-in could not find an opener. Eventually we spotted one fixed to a counter and served ourselves.

We had chosen dishes that seemed quick and simple, because we were tired and faced a long drive home. Every half hour that we waited, piped music played us 'As Time Goes By'. When food eventually came we were almost too weary to eat. Lesley's trout was splayed out on her plate, looking as if someone had stepped on it and bandaged it with slices of ham.

That restaurant summed up one aspect of our experience of Andalusia. Customers waited calmly without grumbling or filling the time by drinking excessively. Stand-in staff coped with unfamiliar jobs as best they could, and it probably never occurred to them to provide a restricted menu and speed turnover. Andalusia is not a place where people get het up. At the first hint of agitation, there is always someone who pats a shoulder and murmurs: '*Tranquilo.*'

CHAPTER TEN

FLAVOURS
OF SPAIN

DAVID PAUSED BEFORE ANSWERING. We had invited him and Dorothy to lunch and asked whether there were foods to avoid. 'We don't eat a lot of meat,' he said. 'We used to be vegetarians but ... well ... the black pudding here is so good I couldn't resist it.'

We first met them in a food shop. Marsha, our New Yorker friend, was shopping with Andrew when she looked up from a shelf of canned tuna and gasped: 'Dorothy!' They had not met for years, not since Marsha was administrator of the Orange Tree theatre in Richmond. Dorothy White is an actress and David Dry, an architect, had worked for the theatre. Settling near Órgiva, they had built their own house on a rise above olive trees, amidst the natural rock garden of the dry land. They had discovered that to eat well in the Alpujarra you have to eat the produce of the land.

We found our own diet changing too, partly because we wanted to learn about local food, but also because the ingredients in the market were those of the traditional Mediterranean diet. There is more meat now, but oil, garlic, fresh vegetables and fish remain the mainstays. Even things that looked familiar tasted and cooked differently. Flavours were strong and satisfying in a way that was new to us.

Órgiva has two markets, the weekly one in the river bed and the everyday covered market in the town centre. The covered market is not a pretty building: concrete and utilitarian, its stalls are on two floors arranged around a patio. The fountain at the centre did not work. On the lower level were meat and fish stalls, for rough-and-ready butchery and small fish from the over-exploited Mediterranean, mainly sardines and anchovies with a few round fish cut into steaks.

Meat meant pork. If we wanted an alternative, we had to specify it. Anyway, pork was the best choice because it was flavoursome, moist and tender. Lambs were slaughtered young, so the chops were a mere mouthful and a leg was scarcely enough for two people. Beef was not to be had, only veal. But not white veal: calves were kept until they were about a year old. The meat was red. This was best stewed slowly with vegetables as it lacked flavour and was frequently tough. The idea of hanging meat to allow it to develop flavour and tenderness was unheard of and cuts were unlike those offered by British, American or French butchers. You have to be careful ordering in restaurants. A waiter misheard Lesley's request for *chuleta* and produced *chuleton*. The difference was half an acre of veal and 300 pesetas.

No, in the Alpujarra meat means pork and every bit of the pig is used. Links of purple-black *morcilla*, rich red *chorizos*, and a dozen other varieties of sausage, hung behind the counters. And everywhere there were hams, air-cured mountain hams. But much more of those hams later.

Chorizo, we discovered, was not one type of sausage but a whole family. The single thing they had in common was flavouring with pimenton, powdered red pepper. Cookery books translate it as paprika but the Collins dictionary hedges its bets and also offers cayenne pepper. Pimenton is neither. It has its own distinct flavour, that of Spain. There are two varieties, hot or sweet. It flavours soups, stews and sausages. The cured *chorizos* are sliced and eaten cold while semi-cured and fresh ones are used in cooking. A few pieces transform a simple soup into a spicy dish for the coldest night. *Chorizo* is the essence of peasant food, preserved with spices for long life and with a robust flavour that disguises the paucity of the meat ration in the family meal.

Most stalls on the upper level of the market sold fruit and vegetables. Tomatoes measured inches across, were misshapen and partly green. Mari Carmen automatically selected the ripest for us. She was used to the ways of foreigners. An attractive dark-haired woman, she was friendly, smiled a lot and was a useful source of information. It helped that she spoke a less strongly accented Spanish. We became regulars at her stall.

We asked her: 'Why do the Spanish prefer greener tomatoes?'

'They are better for salads. When they are all red they are for cooking.'

We followed her advice. Greenish tomatoes were excellent in salads and patchy ones made tasty sauces. They were very different to anything we had eaten before. The flesh was firm, not watery, there were fewer seeds, and the skin was tough. When Lesley skinned tomatoes to make *gazpacho*, the cold Andalusian soup, she used a potato peeler – they were firm enough for that. We devoured a lot of them.

Vegetables came in season and generally from within twenty-five miles of where we lived. We learned to be tactful in our shopping.

'I'd like avocados, please.' Andrew's eyes had fallen on thick fleshy ones.

Mari Carmen offered him a choice. 'Those are from the coast but the small ones are local.'

'Six of the local ones and a lettuce.'

'The lettuces are organic. No artificial fertilizers. My husband grew them on our *finca*.'

'And the broad beans? Are they good today?'

'*Estupendo*.'

And they were. With our heavy olive oil, garlic, a sprig of thyme picked from the hillside and an ounce or two of local ham, they made a fine dish. *Habas con jamon*, an Alpujarran favourite.

Of course, we never had to buy oranges or lemons. Lying in bed we would watch the orange tree outside our window, the early morning light playing on it. As the first sun rays struck, it was as if someone had thrown a switch to light bulbs inside each dangling fruit. We were old enough to remember the excitement when oranges appeared in the greengrocers' shops of post-war Britain. They arrived tenderly wrapped in tissue. Some were buffed to glow on display among the cabbages and apples, but often they sold out before then. Later, when exotic fruits from around the world became commonplace, the orange remained special, that childhood memory of sweet-sharp juice staying with us.

And now we had 135 trees bowed down with fruit. We acquired an electric juicer and drank juice for breakfast and through the day, sometimes mixed with sparkling wine for a treat. Pausing while working in the olive grove, we plucked oranges from a bough and quenched our thirst. We learned which varieties were full of pips and which were full of juice. Lesley made jellies and invented chocolate puddings flavoured with orange. We scraped the zest to flavour stews. But there is not much more you can do with oranges.

Discussing what to do with our glut, we revived an earlier idea: perfect juicy fruit untainted by artificial insecticides or fertilizers, would fetch a premium price in London health food shops. Gradually we realized the truth that had stopped us pursuing this earlier. We had no wish to become fruit merchants and enter a labyrinth of paperwork. The oranges allowed us time to decide. Once ripe they can stay on the trees for up to six months, getting sweeter, until you have to mix the juice with lemon because it has become sickly. We put off decisions.

Meanwhile, Andrew worked on his vegetable garden. This patch became his private place, something that is important for a town dweller: the space to be alone, disturbed only by bird song. To one side of the plot, the land dropped steeply to the dry bed of a small stream. Occasionally water struggled through the golden-brown dust as excess irrigation water was directed back towards the Guadalfeo from a neighbour's land. From both of our terraces we could step out into open country and walk freely among meadow flowers, hundreds of yards to the river or miles up the valley.

'I think the seeds need water,' he would say, and he would be gone, perhaps for hours. After a few minutes contemplating his shoots of garlic, curiosity would lead him across the dry stream and away. Once he climbed up to the almond grove on the top of the crag above the river and found the remains of a fort. He decided it was from the Civil War because the river had been the front line for two years.

Lesley worked out the twisting plot of her next novel while she wandered each day among the trees, ostensibly gathering windfalls. That task too was likely to end with a stroll out over the abandoned land. It was a luxury, having this time and space, the freedom to wander away and think.

José was making progress with the pool. He became part of our life, playing with the kittens, bringing goldfish for our pond. It was he who diagnosed Cosmo as having worms and told Lesley where to find the pet shop and what to ask for. She recited the sentence to the shopkeeper. The woman looked horrified, echoing '*Lombrices?*' Then she clutched her stomach.

'No, *parasitos*.' Everyone in the shop had a good laugh. Locally *lombrices* meant only earthworms.

José was a kind and helpful man, but such a busy one that his instructions to us were comic as well as peremptory. One day Lesley was told rather curtly that she was not to use his cement mixer. Another time he warned her off walking near the pool while he used a tile cutter. 'Too dangerous, this machine,' he insisted. But he showed no inclination to wear protective clothing or, indeed, anything but shorts.

The trouble was that he was like a character in *The Borrowers*. 'Where's the broom?' Lesley would ask. Translated that means: 'Andrew, you have used it again and not put it back where it belongs.'

While José was working, Andrew was safe. 'I'll see if José has it.' And that was where it would be, usually with the handle broken and covered in cement. Exasperation reached a peak one evening when we heard water rushing towards us. Because of the water shortage, sewage was being mixed with the irrigation water. Officially it was treated but that seemed to amount to no more than a sieve which stopped the lumps getting through. Once before, dirty water had arrived at night and leaked into the pool through the half-repaired cracks. José had left instructions that the land around the pool should not be watered and now sewage was again on its way towards his repairs.

But where was the *azadon*? Andrew had to cope with a shovel, a poor tool for switching the direction of a torrent to the abandoned land. Next day he found the *azadon*, its handle snapped. James, who was working with José, was the peacemaker. He was always sent to plead for the loan of tools or to apolog-

87

ize for others taken without permission. He was an Englishman who had travelled the world for twenty-five years with his belongings in a back-pack. His wife went with him. We first saw Elena when she brought his lunch. Drifting through the olive grove dressed in her flowing white silk dress, she looked like a character from a Hardy novel. She was a slight figure, quiet in her movements, like a cat. In greeting or farewell, she put her hands together in front of her face and bowed her head. She was born in South America and spoke four languages.

When José's speed of delivery overran his English, Elena translated from German for us. 'He says these Spanish materials are no good. He must get others from Germany.'

CHAPTER ELEVEN

THE GARDENERS

OUR ALMONDS and peaches blossomed, positively blowsy after the discreet cream flowers of the olive trees. But we were warned not to hold out much hope of enjoying our own peaches, because the trees were notoriously susceptible to attack by insects. Sally, the owner, did not want insecticides used on her land and we preferred not to.

Alternative methods of warding off fruit fly were a major topic at the first meeting we attended of the trees group. It met once a month at a hotel on the edge of Órgiva, the Alpujarra Grill, known colloquially as the *Empalme*, junction.

All its members were incomers, mostly from northern Europe but there was one Spanish couple. They were making gardens or revitalizing farms with the fervour of the Moors a millennium earlier. 'Do you know that according to the Koran, paradise is a dark green luxuriant garden with a river running through it?' asked a German woman who had bought a farm. Considered from a hot, dry country, this seems absolutely right. When the temperature rises above 100°F, heaven on earth is a shady green place with running water. That is what members of the group were creating for themselves through tough, back-breaking and repetitious work. They loved it and found it utterly rewarding.

There was a lengthy discussion about what would grow beneath various trees, how to eliminate weeds and where to obtain plants. The most tenacious weed was a thick stemmed grass called *caniota*. The remedy was eternal vigilance and a ready *azadon*. Desirable plants could be bought near Granada or on the coast where there was a wider selection, although coastal varieties sometimes proved too tender for the severe climate of the Alpujarra. Clearly we had fallen among experts.

Andrew ventured a question. 'How can we prevent insects spoiling our peaches?'

A clamour of helpful voices answered him. Everyone knew how to control fruit fly. They all agreed we should hang old soft drinks bottles from the branches.

'But what should we put in them?'

Dissent broke out. Recipes came thick and fast, with one ingredient standing out as the most important. Human urine. Several voices insisted: 'It attracts the flies, they fall into the bottles and drown.'

Someone else suggested a refinement. 'Add honey, it makes it more effective.'

Well possibly, but a recipe needs to be more specific than that. What exactly were we to do and, equally crucial, when were we to do it? Advice was to hand. 'If you do it too early in the season the mixture loses its efficacy before the flies are laying their eggs.'

More advice followed: 'And if you leave it too late, the grubs will already be growing.'

After spirited discussion, it emerged that no one had yet got it *exactly* right. There was no one whose peaches did not have maggots.

Luckily for us, oranges do not suffer unduly from pests. Ours were perfect, full of astringent juice. Our lemons too were in superabundance. The biggest tree grew handily close to the house so we could pluck a lemon without leaving the patio, whenever we wanted to drop a slice into a gin and tonic, or cut a wedge to squeeze on fish. The only trees we were likely to exhaust were the two mandarin oranges. They ripened rapidly and needed to be eaten without delay. If left, the segments became corky. Stripping our pair of trees, we used what we could ourselves and gave the surplus to a family with a baby. Oranges are good for you but mandarins are better. It is arguable whether they taste nicer, but definite that they contain more vitamin C.

We were not, we discovered, the only people study-ing the state of our trees. One day Antonio brought a stranger to meet us. 'Andrés, this man is a dealer who is buying my crop of oranges. He would like you to sell him yours too.' This, of course, was the other half of fruit farming. No point growing and admiring the stuff if you do not ultimately make an income from it. We had already backed away from exporting oranges, and now here was a chance to sell locally. Andrew conducted negotiations, not because he knew more about the subject but because Lesley had become invisible, the way women always did when an Alpujarran man had the option of speaking to another man.

In this conversation the fruit buyer seemed to have become invisible too. He stood off to the side and let Antonio make his pitch for him. Andrew asked: 'What price is he offering?'

'Twenty-five pesetas a kilo. That's picked and ready for collection at the end of the mule track, mind.'

This was not very promising. We had heard higher prices quoted for previous years. Besides, we were remembering how our olives had weighed less than Spanish-owned olives. Another trick? But no, we did not believe that. Antonio would never have been a party to it, and he had accepted twenty-five pesetas per kilo for his own crop.

Andrew scuffed the dry soil with the toe of his shoe and agreed to think about the offer. Once Antonio had led the silent man away, we sat on the sun-warmed wall by the patio and discussed it. It did not take long. At £125 a ton, or five and a half pence a pound, to us it was not worth the effort. We decided to carry on as we were, using plenty ourselves and giving generously to friends.

Later we wished we had given them away to someone prepared to pick them at that price, but at the time we had different priorities. For one thing, we doubted whether we could control a grove full of fruit-pickers. How would we get them to leave anything for us? And we did want some fruit left on the trees, for the sheer joy of seeing oranges hanging there.

Our other reason had much to do with an incident a week earlier. It was twilight and we had stirred our log fire, shut our shutters and made ourselves cosy for an evening's reading. Suddenly we heard the sound. Something was shuffling towards us, something was being dragged.

Andrew giggled nervously: 'It's like the sound effects of an old horror film.'

'Is it human or animal?'

'What sort of human makes a sound like that?'

We opened a shutter and tried looking along the patio but a loquat tree blocked our view. Andrew opened the door, poised to slam it shut again if necessary. He saw movement in the shadows near the bathroom. Out he went, Lesley peering from behind.

There on our patio was Charles Manson. Well, anyway it looked like him. Black eyes glared from matted hair and beard. He continued to weave towards us. Andrew believed he was actually a British hippy left over from the seventies and spoke to him in English. No good. The man was Spanish. As he came into the lamp light we made out the sack flung over his ragged clothes and the other sack he was dragging.

'Where's the river?' he asked.

'This isn't the path, it's back up that way.' Andrew pointed into the dusk.

A sniff. 'Can I go through this way?'

'No, you have to go back up the track and turn left.'

He was reluctant, Andrew insistent. In the end he trundled back up the patio, pulling his sack along: two steps and drag, two steps and drag . . .

Another evening we were sitting on the patio when

we saw a backpack and a pair of legs passing our bedroom and disappearing down the slope beneath the washing line. The visitor was Irish. She also wanted to reach the river, and had been given directions to avoid the path and traipse through our place instead. Understandable if it had been a short cut, but it was appreciably longer.

Realizing the mule track led straight up our patio, the Irish girl had taken a considerate detour. 'I didn't want to disturb you so I went round behind the house.' We plunged into our routine explanation about the decent path that led down to the river, and about the vulnerability of Andrew's vegetable patch. Ever since people had set up camp in the broad riverbed of the Guadalfeo, we had been finding footprints among our vegetables and flowers.

The Irish girl, like others before her, promised to spread the word that walkers bound for the camp should take the path over the abandoned land, not advance down our mule track. Perhaps she did, but the damage had been done. Each person who plunged down on to the lower terrace followed the line of trampled grass. The repetition was creating a path, and a path meant it was harder to convince people there was *not* a path.

Sometimes, when people spotted us having lunch on the patio, they skirted behind the house, or we spotted them dodging through the trees. Others saw no reason to veer and marched straight through. The cats hated it, especially as walkers were frequently accompanied by dogs. In a couple of cases, by many dogs.

Lesley glanced out of the kitchen window one day

while Posy was feeding and saw the cat perform cartoon antics: an overstated arching of the spine and then she was a horizontal black streak. Dashing outside Lesley was overwhelmed by half a dozen dogs coming full tilt. Their owner, an Englishwoman, was annoyed.

'They were all right until they saw that cat. I was trying to take them this way.' She gestured to the bank behind the house.

'That's not the way to the river.'

'Oh, it's all right, I always take them over your roof. It won't disturb you.'

It seemed pointless to argue with this one. Her dogs were already scrabbling among the vegetables.

Posy had disappeared. Cosmo was torn between flight and motherly duties. Kittens cowered in dark corners. Their tea chest was near the bathroom, and as the door was usually open, they had a bolthole. Whenever strangers, human or animal, appeared it was a safe bet that five kittens had sought sanctuary there. While the dogs were still within earshot, we did a quick head count. Three in the boiler cupboard and a couple under the sink. Good. Cosmo patrolled the low wall skirting the patio, on guard. She knew they were all safe, because she was not giving the throaty 'come here' call she used to round up wanderers.

Lesley went calling for Posy, on the edge of the abandoned land. Sometimes we saw rollers, cattle egrets or bee eaters out there, and occasionally an eagle, high and drifting upriver. The earth was tawny, a large black cat should be fairly obvious. A tabby, stripy and patched like Cosmo, would be perfectly disguised, ideal for hunting. But there were no cats, only dogs barking far off.

Towards evening, when she went to the pool to check the water level and see whether José's repair was working, Lesley happened to glance up into one of our great olive trees and there, right up near the top, was a pair of green eyes. Posy came smoothly down the trunk, sleek and black and unscathed. That time she was lucky.

Andrew used a dead tree to plug a gap in the hedge near the vegetable patch. Footprints led up to it. Next day the tree had been cast aside. He replaced it. It was moved again. One night we were woken by feet rampaging over the roof, another there were frightful screams from the cats, a commotion. Next morning the dead tree had vanished completely and so had Posy. The vegetable patch was churned up, the plants obliterated.

Andrew erected a barricade of branches and canes at the gap and placed a makeshift gate across the mule track. No one could any longer trot out the excuse that they thought they were on a path to or from the river. All too late, of course. The vegetable plot had been destroyed. Worse, it had ceased to be a private place.

And that was why we shied away from inviting fruit-pickers. Too many strangers were tramping around already, we could not face any more.

So we let the oranges stay on the trees until they became unpalatably sweet and soft, and then we let them fall and rot. It was wasteful and in time the windfalls attracted flies, which was bad too. But we were not the only people deterred from selling their oranges that spring because of the low price. Commercial growers of Valencia dumped thousands of tons. By the time it reaches a British shop, a Spanish orange costs ten times what the grower was paid. Who benefits? A British truck driver offered a clue: the only load that was so profitable it was worth driving an empty lorry to fetch, was Spanish oranges for the Christmas market.

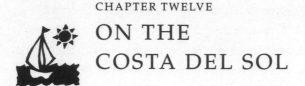 ON THE COSTA DEL SOL

MONTSE WAS FINDING THE CONCEPT hard to understand. 'A sandwich of fried potatoes?'

'Yes. With butter.'

'Ugh!' She paused, doubt on her face, not sure whether to believe this revelation of English taste. 'What did you say you call it?'

'A chip butty. It's very popular in the north of England.' Andrew watched the incredulity on his Spanish teacher's face and wondered if he had gone too far this time. Butter, in the land of olive oil, put it well beyond the bounds of probability. Working as a teacher in a language school on the Costa del Sol, Montse had seen something of the way the English colony lived. Some of them, she maintained, could not speak a word of Spanish after fifteen years in the town. Even so, a sandwich of fried potatoes and butter was beyond her comprehension.

Andrew had settled the dates for his month-long intensive Spanish course soon after we heard when Lesley's mother would be visiting. He said he wanted Lesley to be alone in the vulnerable house as little as possible. And that was how he came to be discussing eating habits with Montse in Nerja, one of the smarter towns on the southern coast. He was still amused by it when he set off to find his evening meal. If he stayed on the waterside or in the town centre, he was in the land of international menus for tourists. By heading for the quieter, disregarded streets he could find bars and restaurants where the food and the language were Spanish, and so were the prices. He walked on, past the German beer cellar signs, past the pub and the grub signs. And then he saw it.

Next day he told Montse and the class that there were at least two English pubs in Nerja where they could sample chip butties. He does not think any of them braved it, although a couple of Montse's colleagues took him aside and begged help in perfecting their pronunciation of *cheep booty*. He may not have expanded their culinary experience, but he had given them a hilarious anecdote.

Presumably few of the resident English population – there are perhaps 200,000 on the Costa del Sol and hundreds of thousands more during the holidays – want to eat chip butties regularly, but the availability reinforced a stereotype.

It is more or less possible to live on the *costa* and ignore Spain. You need not learn the language, or understand anything about the way the country works. You can watch satellite television in English, shop in a supermarket that stocks British brands and buy English newspapers. If you want to discover how fellow expatriates enjoy life on the *costa*, then you can read the newspapers and magazines produced locally in your mother tongue.

We heard many people say they would prefer to be in Britain if they could have the sunshine and cheap wine. Sometimes it was a joke and sometimes not. Others admitted they would prefer it even without those benefits. It seemed a great pity that they were not enjoying Spain more, that in so many ways they were not really *in* Spain. Whatever they had hoped for, they had become stuck in an ersatz country.

Andrew had first seen the Costa del Sol thirty years before spending his month at Nerja. At that time, there were only a few hotels scattered along the coast and workmen were starting to blast the road that made possible the massive tourist development. He remembers sitting on a headland and seeing nothing but fishing boats and a distant village, white houses spilling down to the sea. Now, much of the narrow coastal strip between mountains and sea is a ribbon of flats, hotels, bars, restaurants, discos and housing developments. Golf courses are daubs of alien green. The *costa* caters for many tastes, although it can no longer satisfy the lovers of lonely headlands and empty shores. Marbella, for instance, has the look and feel of a Californian town, while the apartment blocks of Torrox put us in mind of bits of Liverpool or south London.

We were luckier in our local stretch of coast, now named the Costa Tropical by a tourist industry keen to distinguish it from the rest of the Costa del Sol. The road from Órgiva brought us out close to the delightful town of Salobreña. Flat roofed white houses climb the hill to a Moorish castle. Turn east along the coast and the resorts are Spanish. Go west and you are heading for an international mix. Generally we stopped in Salobreña or headed east, because we had come to Spain to experience the country, its people, its food, and its life. We were seeking a change, new experiences. We even acquired a preference for olive oil on our toast instead of butter.

In the Alpujarra there was not always such an option. There was the local way of doing things and that was that. We rather enjoyed not having to make endless choices, the way we were obliged to in restaurants or shops in London. Incomers either accepted that they were playing by local rules or they grew frustrated and soon moved down to the coast. While we lived near Órgiva there was not one shop or bank where you could hope to use anything but Spanish, there were no signs in any other language.

There was a bar though. The Obelix, the bar they used to call the German bar, the one the Grundies told us about, the one people had originally hoped we would call in at, but which we had avoided. The *Guardia* used it as a pool of interpreters when they had to deal with non-Spanish miscreants. Once they asked Andrew to help them, misled about the quality of his Spanish!

While we were around, the German manager turned into a Belgian one who turned into an American woman and her British partner. All of them kept the menu in Spanish, all the signs and notices too. It

was safe to assume their customers knew enough of
the language and preferred it that way. If not, they
could make for the coast.

The English have been in love with the Costa del
Sol for more than a hundred years. A late nineteenth-
century edition of Richard Ford's *Handbook for Travellers in Spain* recommended Málaga where the climate
was 'one of the most equitable in Europe . . . Winter,
in our sense of the term, is almost unknown.' And he
was most reassuring that visitors need not cope with
Spanish food and wine. 'Málaga is supplied with first-
rate bottled ale by Mr Hodgson, Puerta del Mar, next
door to the Fonda de la Alameda, at whose establish-
ment English goods and provisions of all kinds can
be obtained.'

For us, Málaga meant the airport on its outskirts.
We were not quite as unfamiliar with it as the passengers who sat next to us on one flight and mused
that in the twenty-four years they had been visiting
the *costa* they had never once been into Málaga. Our
own glimpses of the city were cursory, snatched as
we fetched family and friends from the airport or
delivered them to it. One day the timing was so awkward that rather than drive the five hour round trip
on consecutive days we booked into a hotel near the
bus station and set aside hours to explore.

We went to the cemetery. The Protestant cemetery,
which lies at the foot of the castle hill, tells tales of
nineteenth-century visitors, some perhaps lured to
Málaga by Mr Ford's enthusiasm. A green and quiet
place, the graves attest to failed cures, and desperate
parents seeking recovery for invalid children. It was
created in 1830 by the British consul, William Mark, a

102

man who encouraged his fellow countrymen to visit Málaga, this 'second paradise'. Spain, though, had made the journey to the first paradise difficult for Protestants. It classified them as infidels and denied them burial in consecrated ground. At Málaga they were planted feet forwards on the beach.

We presented ourselves at the heavy iron gates and called through. This excited the gatekeeper's Alsatian dog whose bark obliterated our request for entry and his master's orders to be quiet. But after a lot of noise we were inside. The dog subsided, the gatekeeper resumed his more interesting job of tending the pot plants he sold, and we wandered off among the memorials. It was a poignant place, crowded with people who chose to live out their years in a country they loved; and with invalids who trusted their health to the wonderful climate; and with mariners who came to grief far from home.

We found the gravestone of Gamel Woolsey, that sensitive writer whose book *Death's Other Kingdom* is one of the finest pieces of writing about the Civil War. She married Gerald Brenan, after his Alpujarra phase, and they lived in Churriana, a village now overwhelmed by Málaga airport. Her epitaph, lines from *Cymbeline*, is apt for all who share her resting place:

> Fear no more the heat o' the sun
> Nor winter's furious rages.

Brenan does not occupy the plot reserved there for him. He left his body for medical research at Málaga.

You can be buried in that cemetery these days but the remains of most Britons who die on the *costa* are airlifted to English country churchyards or suburban crematoria. That is the only way some dare return home. Frank was one of those. Andrew met him in the home of a frequently unemployed Spanish waiter where Andrew lodged during his month in Nerja.

The town sits on low cliffs above the sandy beaches and rocky coves overlooked by the Balcony of Europe, the headland in the town centre. Hotels and housing developments do not dominate. Nerja is a place for sitting at pavement cafés and watching people go by. Jorge, the waiter, lived with his wife, Encarnación, two teenage daughters and a son, in an old house amidst the jumble of streets. Encarnación held the family together, kept the house clean and the children well-dressed. To help she took lodgers from the language school and gripped the purse tight. She shopped wisely in the market and cooked well.

Andrew chose to live with a family rather than in a flat or *pension* because it forced him to practise his Spanish. The morning he met Frank he was woken early by people in the living-room below. Downstairs he discovered Jorge and another man on the settee, a bottle of *aguadente* on the table before them. Encarnación hovered in the kitchen, nervous and unsmiling.

'You're English?' slurred the stranger.

'Yes.'

'I'm Frank. We've had a good night. We're pissed.'

'Where are you from?' An unnecessary question. The Essex accent was plain despite the slurring. Frank was an emaciated man with pock-marked skin and long lank fair hair. He was in his forties.

'Rayleigh.'

Encarnación came in and, forcing a smile, asked Andrew what he would like for breakfast.

'Just a black coffee, please.'

'No toast?'

He said no. All he could think of was making the fastest escape. Yet Frank insisted on talking. 'You living in Spain?'

'Yes. How long have you been here?'

'Thirteen years.'

'You must like it.'

'Hate it. Jorge's my good friend. We go out an' get pissed to forget.'

'You'd rather be back in England, than here?'

''Course.'

'Why don't you go then?'

'Can't.'

'Why not?'

Silence.

The coffee came. Andrew gulped it down and fled.

We do not know the exact story of Frank. We can guess, though, because many people on the fringes of society back home build new lives on the coast, often becoming respectable members of the community. A friend of ours remarked of one notorious criminal: 'All I can say is he's always been very nice to me.'

Lesley choked on her drink. 'But *you* weren't driving a security van!'

The subject also came up the day she went to Reading prison to talk about crime fiction. The session was being recorded by the BBC and once that part was over she approached one of the inmates. He was well read and had made significant contributions to the discussion. 'Robert, I'm sure I've seen you before.'

They worked out that they had been on the same flight to Málaga a year before, when we were making our first visit to the Alpujarra. He spent much of his time on the Costa del Sol, spoke and read Spanish. We remembered the flight well. We had joked that half the passengers on this mid-week scheduled flight looked like criminals and the other half like policemen.

At Reading Robert wore brown trousers instead of blue, the sign of the man on remand awaiting trial. He had mentioned earlier that much of his reading had been done 'in places like this'. He gave a roguish wink. 'I'm an international car thief, aren't I? Well, they haven't actually proved it yet.'

CHAPTER THIRTEEN

FIT FOR
A KING?

MOTHERS HAVE A KNACK of humiliating their children with a few words but none have done it so famously as Ayeshah to her son Boabdil, King of Granada. It happened as the royal retinue straggled towards exile in the Alpujarra. When they reached a low hill of red soil which gives the last view of the city, Boabdil turned and cried. Ayeshah was caustic. 'You do well to weep like a woman for that you have not defended like a man.'

We were talking about this story as we drove home from an exhibition of Spanish Islamic art in the Alhambra.

'Do you know what King Charles V said when he heard it?' Andrew asked. ' "She spake well. Better a

tomb in the Alhambra than a palace in the Alpujarra."
But where was the palace in the Alpujarra?'

'No idea. It probably sank back into the earth long
ago.'

Curious, we tried to find out. Guide books and
tourist leaflets were vague. After all, Boabdil spent
only nine months in the Alpujarra, hunting with his
falcons and greyhounds, before being forced out of
Spain altogether. His hawks had stooped on their prey
in the mountains of the eastern Alpujarra, many miles
from our olive grove. But it was unclear exactly where
all this hawking and hunting had gone on. Different
sources suggested different places, and none of them
mentioned whether there was anything left of the
palace he had come down to after relinquishing the
Alhambra. Was it true he had lived at Andarax?
Cobda? Codbaa? Fondón? Or Presidio?

If we had been more familiar with the eastern Alpujarra, we would have untangled it sooner. But to us it
was deeply confusing because few of the names
appear on present day maps. We wondered about lost
villages, a plausible solution in an area that had been
severely depopulated. The truth was odder because, in
a way, all the sources were correct. Trawling through
Spanish books Andrew pieced the story together.
Briefly, it was this. In 1924 the village of Presidio had
been renamed Fuente Victoria in honour of Queen
Victoria Eugenia, wife of Alfonso III, deposed by the
Republic which in turn fell to Franco's rebels. In Moorish times the same village had been Cobda, alterna-
tively spelled Codbaa. It lies in the valley of the river
Andarax, a mile from the town of Laujar de Andarax,
but in the municipality of the more distant Fondón.

We planned a mooch through the mountains and villages of that other Alpujarra but we delayed, interrupted by visitors and by writing. And then one day we opened a fat new guide book that claimed that Boabdil's palace still existed. We went to see for ourselves.

Fuente Victoria was celebrating the day of its patron, the Virgin of the Angels, when we arrived. It was mid-afternoon, the quiet time of a fiesta as people were at home taking siestas, gathering strength for the evening. A handful of men hung around in the square chatting with barmen who had little to do. Others were installing the sound system which would blast the village later. Along the main road stall holders waited for stray customers, and teenagers sat idly on the wall of a burbling *acequia*. In a park a mother restrained her toddler from running into a pond.

On the edge of the village stood what looked like a huge oil storage tank, but low and painted red. This was the travelling bull ring, erected for the big night of the fiesta. A van with loudspeakers drove past, deafening in its appeals for people to buy tickets. That evening we saw two solemn men in suits of lights dashing out of a bar on their way to the ring.

Away from the main road, the noise of the loudspeakers was subdued, and once the van had gone to trouble other villages, it was totally quiet. A black cat with green eyes like Posy's crossed the road in front of us. Nothing else moved. In the shadowy white streets the full heat of the sun was held at bay. Ahead lay the church. Like most in this area it had been a mosque in Boabdil's time. Before the Moors arrived in Spain it may have been a Christian church, and before that possibly a Roman temple. The Romans had built a fortress here when they came to mine the gold of the Alpujarra.

We walked around the outside of the church. At the back a cracked and weathered building joined it at right angles. Peering through windows into large rooms, empty and derelict, we spotted some old olive mill stones stored there.

Moving on, we noticed that one of the great double doors of the building was open. A woman, with the papery skin of extreme old age, was sitting inside, in shadow. Her chair was dilapidated, her dull eyes unfocused. An aluminium walking frame suggested she was unable to move much. Andrew leaned towards her. A slight movement of her head acknowledged his *'Buenos dias'*.

'Is this,' he asked, 'the old palace?'

A ridiculous question. Beyond her we could see a modern sink and cooker in a ruined patio. The place was no one's idea of a palace!

She was uncomprehending. 'What?'

Andrew tried again: 'Did Boabdil live here?'

She moved her head with a soft *'si'*.

So we had found it. The last palace of the last Moorish king in Spain. Andrew asked whether we might go into the patio, a question he had to repeat and more loudly. Lesley went through, anxious for a glimpse before we were turned away. Then a younger woman entered the patio from a door at the side. She had the implacable face we often noticed in the eastern Alpujarra, but agreed without hesitation that we might look.

We had an impression of cracked pink marble columns linked by a washing line that appeared to be all that held them up; clothes pegged out to dry; a sagging wooden gallery; sunlight pouring in where part of the roof had collapsed; and another chunk looking ready to descend, red tiles teetering above us. Plastic crates of potatoes, beans, onions, green peppers, oranges and peaches filled one corner. The palace had become a greengrocer's shop, it had the earthy warm smell of one.

The silence was awkward. Andrew tried to stimulate conversation, asking the woman to confirm what seemed absurd. 'This was where King Boabdil lived?'

'Yes.'

'And you live here now, do you?'

'Yes.' A pause, then she gestured to the door she had come through. 'In that part.'

It was hard to know what to say. Once upon a time it had been a fine building, surviving details such as the capitals of the columns showed that. In truth it was never a *palacio* but a *palacete*, meaning a house fitted for a local lord. Kings who have lost a kingdom do not have a lot of choice.

That terrible silence again. Andrew struggled to say something. He plumped for the wrong thing. 'It's magnificent.'

The Spanish past tense had deserted him. The woman looked at him as if he were mad.

He blundered on. 'It's a crime it's in this state.'

Silence.

He sought an escape, from this awkwardness and from the place itself. 'May I buy some fruit?'

'Of course.' Why else does one go to the greengrocer?

'Two peaches.'

In Spain you do not buy two peaches. She gave him a hard look as she bent over the crate. Quickly he changed the order. 'No, four . . . I mean a kilo.'

We paid for them, a pittance for admission to the palace of Boabdil. They were awful peaches, the hard flavourless clingstone type. After crunching through a couple, we tossed the rest away.

Lurching from old to new, we stayed overnight in a Laujar hotel that was only two days old. Its restaurant had not opened at all so we went into town. Spurning a free bus ride to the bullfight, we followed the trail of picnickers to a beauty spot, the source of the river Andarax. There were barbecue grills beneath the trees; large family parties showing every sign of quiet enjoyment; a couple of bars; and a bone dry gully beside a notice that announced: 'Fishing is forbidden.'

Next morning the hotel owner did not want to take our money. Then he asked a sum so low that Andrew persuaded him to accept more. The hotel was too new to have its rates fixed by the authorities. Altogether, our Boabdil trip had been full of quirky incident.

When Boabdil left the Alpujarra he settled in Fez, attempted to build in the style of the Alhambra, and died in battle in 1536 fighting to defend someone else's kingdom. One of the exhibits in the exhibition we had seen at the Alhambra was reputed to be his sword, surrendered at the battle of Lucena, north east of Granada, in 1483. The sumptuous filigree and inlay work echoed the patterns of the plasterwork of the Alhambra.

We queued for four hours to see the al-Andalus

exhibition, frustrated by queue-jumping coach-parties. Weeks later the system was changed so that tour groups no longer took precedence. Even without a major exhibition occupying half the building, the Alhambra has a serious problem. After centuries of neglect, it suffers from too much attention. For the sake of the fabric of the building, as well as the comfort of sightseers, visitors were limited to batches of 200 each half hour.

The day we queued was one of the first on which we had time to behave like tourists. The exhibition brought together the finest examples of Spanish Islamic art from museums in fifteen countries. As for the building itself, we tended to agree with Sacheverell Sitwell who wrote: 'Why is it that the Alhambra with so many beauties, is a little boring; that the first sight of its interior is better than the second or the tenth . . .?' In the end, after taking many visitors, we disagreed with him. The Alhambra was more rewarding on each visit as we came to appreciate an unfamiliar art.

Its gardens, the oldest in Europe, brought to mind the Koran's description of Paradise we had heard at the trees group: 'A dark green luxuriant garden with a river running through it, planted with fruit trees, pomegranates and palms.' There, in the gardens of the Generalife summer palace, Boabdil's wife met her lover in the shade of a cypress tree. The king was not a lucky man.

CHAPTER FOURTEEN

HARD
ROADS

A MAKESHIFT TENT appeared on the abandoned land, close to us. Andrew dashed back from his early morning amble to break the news. We did not see how it could possibly be good news; there had been so many tales of camps springing up where no one but the campers wanted them. One woman could no longer walk her dogs down to the river because travellers blocked the path. Another woman living alone was intimidated into paying campers to do odd jobs, when all she wanted was for them to move their tents and old vans from her doorstep.

We were exchanging misgivings when James, who was working on the pool with José, popped out from the plastic sheet. Elena followed.

Apparently they had quarrelled with the owner of

114

the caravan they had been living in. A few days later the owner stopped Lesley in town and asked her to pass on a message. 'Tell them it's time to eat humble pie. Send them back to the caravan.' Expunging humble pie, Lesley started delivering a more tactful version. She was interrupted by dismissive laughter. No, the caravan was out, they preferred to stay where they were. We held our breath and waited to see how soon others would join them. Andrew muttered about thin ends of wedges.

Meanwhile, they folded their things neatly in the day, left vulnerable stuff in bags hung from a tree, and became as much a feature of the scene as the goats that trotted past.

During the olive harvest, we had put out our cuttings for the herd. That was how we came to know Ramon. He was the herdsman we saw most often, walking his foraging flock through the terraces and along the river bed. By local standards it was a big flock, 140-strong, and he told us he kept even more on the higher mountains. Some days he carried a newborn kid, its two front legs grasped in his hand and the body hanging limply, uncomplaining. Until they have found their feet, these sudden additions to the flock cannot follow as the mothers move on in the search for food.

Ramon would sit for a time, his back to a tree, calling occasionally to his half-dozen dogs, but generally leaving control of the flock to them. Large dogs of no particular breed, they worked quietly and efficiently.

Keeping livestock had become more profitable than growing crops and fruit but it remained a bare and hard way of life. Few people tilled the land or kept animals to earn their living. Older men, like our neighbour Antonio, did but most younger ones were only part-time farmers on the family holdings. Those who wanted to work the land – natives and incomers – could do so in either the new way or the old. But most of the Spanish, even those who continued to plough with mules, found it difficult to understand people like Philip and Christine who would not use insecticide sprays and artificial fertilizers.

Philip had worked in a canning factory and Christine had taught small children. They threw up their jobs, packed their belongings in a van, arrived in the Alpujarra and bought a few acres. They were so sure in their own minds that this was the life they wanted, they left themselves no lifebelt in England. If they had stayed Christine would have been a deputy head in a year and a head in a couple more. Philip's boss told him he had been in line for a shift manager's job and grumbled about money wasted on training.

We met them in Órgiva one market day, one of those bright warm Thursdays when people linger at the tables outside the bars, and acquaintances are made and friendships develop. They said they had come to the Alpujarra six years previously with money for enough land to survive by working through the year. In Britain they could not afford land nor would the weather allow them to work intensively through the four seasons. Christine, who had learned Spanish at school, spoke Castilian as pure as her home counties English, while Philip's Spanish was as rural in tone as his English. Like Gerald Brenan, Philip had learned the language from Alpujarran village people.

Diversity in language is valued now: in the 1930s it was not and Brenan, who wrote among other things a history of Spanish literature, was dropped by the BBC because of the Alpujarran accent in his occasional broadcasts.

The way Christine and Philip spoke, as much as what they said, confirmed that they are happy with their life in Spain. Once we asked an expert in linguistics, a Mongolian by birth who now works at an Israeli university, why some immigrants held on to the accents of their motherlands while others did not.

'It's easy,' he said in his perfect English, 'those who keep the accents of their original countries are those who are not truly settled and dream of returning one day.' In other words, your accent reveals where your heart is.

Christine and Philip invited us to call on them. Directions were precise but, when we came to it, dubious. To find them we had to climb several thousand feet, then forsake good tarmac for dust roads. Typically, these plunge down improbable slopes enfolding one valley and then leap over a ridge into the next, like a switchback ride. At each twist and fall, we saw the white splash of a distant village; or a straggle of trees proving the site of a long-gone house; or golden light glittering along a stream; or the airy mountain ranges below us, a landscape rumpled like a dropped shawl.

At one of the abandoned farms we stopped to explore. The building was stone-built with space for family and animals. Once, its yard-thick walls had been protection from winter cold and summer heat, but by the time we saw it the flat roof had caved in. A beam rested on a broken esparto-seated chair.

Beside it, half-covered by a cascade of launa from the roof, sat a smashed earthenware water pot and next to that a cracked blue plastic bucket. As the house was built into the slope, it was two storeys high at the front but only one at the rear. Inside there were windowless rooms where people had slept and winter food had been stored. Whitewash clung to walls and a candlestick stood on a mantelshelf.

Nearby, on a headland jutting above the valley, we spotted a threshing circle. Grass was growing between the closely laid stones, doing its utmost to disguise it. We speculated on helping the tourist industry by writing that the paved circles littering the hills were the remains of an old religion. We invented gods who came in flying saucers to these ready and waiting landing sites, which were always (the gods being picky about such things) in the most beautiful places. The prosaic explanation was a practical one: threshing circles were made on exposed sites where they catch the winnowing winds. In summer the circles are discs of gold straw.

From our viewpoint on the *era*, which is what these circles are called, we could see a deep green patch of alfalfa. Close to it were poplar trees and the wall of a house, a house that had been whitewashed but made yellow by African dust carried on the wind. That house was our objective. Christine had eyed our jeep and told us: 'Follow the track until you think you've reached the end, but carry on. Most people leave their cars there but you'll be all right in the *todo terreno*.'

When it came to it we were none too confident. The track was heading for nothing. Someone had bull-dozed it along the route of a horseshoe path. Perhaps a Madrid family who dreamed of summer holidays in the family *cortijo* had done it. Or the work could have been part of a provincial government scheme to halt rural depopulation. In the years since, the track had been narrowed by landslips and rain had scooped channels. When we dared take our eyes off the crumbling surface, we saw mountains on the other side of the valley a mile away. Ahead of us there was bound to be a precipice. We inched the car forward. The bonnet rose up until we could see only sky above it. Not liking this at all, we got out. Gingerly peering over the edge, we discovered that within a short distance the track plunged down the mountainside in a series of horribly tight hairpin bends.

Lesley switched the car into four wheel drive and we eased forward. It still looked as though she intended to drive straight up into the sky. Then over the lip, the first of the hairpins rushed towards us. Tyres slithered on loose stones. We paused again, engaged low ratio gears and crept down. And so on, and so down. Rounding the last bend, we drew up next to Philip and Christine's little Renault. How did they do it?

From there on we had to walk. The path carried on zig-zagging down to the valley floor. Andrew hurried on while Lesley stumbled down more slowly, catching at trees and shrubs for support. The river bed was grey and stony and dry. We might have been walking on a pebbly beach. But then Andrew came to one where water flowed. He sat down on a stone and waited, smelling the sweet coconut scent of gorse and watching an eagle circling above.

'*Buenadia.*' Good day was run together as one harsh

word. A short square man appeared over the side of the bank.

'*Buenos dias*. We're going to the house of *Felipe* and *Cristina*.' Then Andrew explained the 'we'. 'My wife's coming. She finds these Spanish *caminos* hard.'

Lesley was lost. Once Andrew sat down she could not work out where he was. Shrubs sprouting from the grey stone obscured everything below elbow height. She tried calling. He seemed to have gone an impossible distance and, as she had been watching where she put her feet rather than watching him, she had no idea in which direction he had gone. When she came to the water she jumped across it. But as the shrubs on the far side were scratchy, she jumped back.

Andrew was introducing himself to the man he had met. 'I'm Andrés.'

'Paco. Fag?' He flicked a blue and white packet of Ducados.

'Thank you.'

At the first puffs of smoke Lesley came picking her way over the stones of the river bed. Paco offered a better route. 'I can take you another way without going through the river.'

It was no better, it was different, that's all. Gorse and brambles snatched at our clothing. Once we had to drop six feet into another boulder-strewn water course. We tramped across Paco's terraces, past his beans and through his almond grove. As we went, he described how he came down from the village every day with his mule to farm. No one else did that any longer. He shared the valley with Philip and Christine, and when the sun went down they had it to themselves.

CHAPTER FIFTEEN

TRAPPED
IN TIME

CHRISTINE AND PHILIP had been to a party the night before and were behind with their work but they welcomed us. Having no telephone they did not expect warning. Random visitors enlivened the routine.

They had used the word fiesta which means anything from having a few friends round for a birthday drink to a national holiday or the local saint's day. The one thing these events have in common is that the best does not happen until the time of evening when in England people look at their watches and mutter about baby-sitters.

Although they had had little sleep, work could not be put off. As she talked to us Christine carried on pasturizing the day's milk to make cheese. Despite the saturating sun, her skin retained a delicate English quality. With her dark hair held back by a scarf, she looked very much the dairy maid.

'What,' we asked her, 'was the fiesta for?'

She adjusted the gas flame beneath the pan. 'Some men shot a wild boar the other day and decided to cook it and have a party.'

'But you're vegetarians!'

'Oh, that was all right. They made a potato omelette for us.'

If you live in the country and make a living from the land you cannot be too dogmatic, you have to balance idealism with practicality. This had been brought home to us in a tricky scene at our house a few weeks earlier. We were having lunch with two vegetarian men. One was Patrick, who had taught us how to harvest olives and was helping with the watering. The other was Tim who had come to the area to run a spiritual retreat centre. The job and the promises that went with it had evaporated and he was doing odd jobs to earn the money to go home. We had long known that a high proportion of the people whom we might feed, by invitation or accident, would be vegetarian and we were careful in what we provided. It became a rule of the house that we used only vegetarian stock cubes so that soups could be conjured up without breaking anyone's taboos.

From time to time Patrick or Tim had been around at lunchtimes and shared our snack, but until this day they had not been there together. As they did not know each other, they had an exploratory kind of conversation. Patrick's organic farming proved a rewarding topic. Then calamity. Tim, who was a strict vegetarian and once kept a health food shop, realized that Patrick, who was a stricter vegetarian and did not eat fish either, reared his goats for the Christmas table. There was a peculiar silence while Tim, spoon poised between soup bowl and mouth, worked out the significance of Patrick earning more money from goats sold in December. We dared not meet each other's eyes. Unable to resist giggles we invented excuses to slip away, fetching more bread, refilling the water jug.

Philip and Christine's omelette at the wild boar feast threatened to lead to yet another discussion of the ethics of vegetarianism, but just then Philip came into the kitchen. 'They've flattened the maize again,' he said. Anyone else bearing his news might have been angry, but he was not like that, facing problems with resignation.

Christine sighed.

'Who have?' we asked.

'The wild boar,' Philip said. 'They've come back into this valley this year.'

'Do they take much?'

'No, the problem isn't what they eat it's the damage they do. By just moving around they can ruin the crops.'

Ideally, they would have preferred it if the wild boar were not hunted. Being practical, they were delighted when those that were troubling them were killed. They drew the ethical line at a different point from Patrick because not only did they refuse to hunt or eat animals but they also refused to rear them for anyone else to eat. And yet farmers, however high-minded, cannot afford sentimentality.

Philip offered an example. 'Did you notice the young cockerel running around outside?'

We had. He was pretty, like a game cock, and he had announced our arrival as enthusiastically as the dogs.

'Well, the old one had to go so we gave him to a woman in the village although we knew she was going to cook him. In return she gave us that smart young fellow you saw strutting around.'

Animals were an essential part of the natural farming cycle. Without the muck from their cow, two mules and the chickens, Philip and Christine would have needed to use artificial fertilizers. Philip had no doubt: intensive agriculture is unsustainable and threatens disaster.

As we walked around their land that afternoon, beside a river flowing with clear water, it was difficult to believe there was a serious drought in Andalusia. Reservoirs were recording record low levels and in Seville, where water supplies were cut for twelve hours a day, buckets and bottles of mineral water were provided in hotel rooms.

In the byre, the lower floor of Philip and Christine's house, Andrew picked up a spare cow bell to hear its flat ring. The cow in the stall mooed urgently, fooled into calling to the one that used to share the byre. Andrew felt ashamed, realizing it was thoughtless not to expect a cow to welcome the return of a companion.

The cow was coming with us to the alfalfa field to eat the stubble where Philip was scything fodder with easy swings. This was to be stored in a ruined house by the threshing circle which he used, riding a sledge behind a circling mule to separate grain from straw.

Their farm was an idyll, trapped in time, until you noticed the solar panel newly fixed to the wall of the house. They had a six inch television, music and light to read by. But there was no light in the byre. That was not allowed under the scheme to provide subsidized solar power. Someone sitting in an air-conditioned office had ruled that people should work by torch light or lantern.

We took home with us a bag of juicy plums. They tasted of sunshine.

Antonio was waiting with news when we parked the car. 'The land is for sale.'

'The abandoned land?' Puzzling. We had been told it was entailed for generations; just how many generations, depended upon who was telling the tale.

'Yes.' Antonio's story was that it had been mortgaged and the loan had not been repaid. Now the bank was selling. 'For £75,000.' The price of property was always important to Antonio. We never found out if this was a true story or another rumour. The abandoned land stayed abandoned.

That evening Posy came home. A bad limp and a wound on a back leg suggested a dog bite. She disappeared again after eating and that became her new pattern. 'Cats do this,' people assured us. 'She'll be back once she's well. It'll be all right, you'll see.' But it wasn't. Not really.

CHAPTER SIXTEEN

FLAMENCO MEETS BAROQUE

STRUGGLING ALONG with his Spanish, Andrew was given a useful tip. 'They use the posh English words.' *Exactamente*. 'Culture' is one of those words. In Britain anyone wanting to bring in the crowds avoids it, but in Spain it has a wider meaning. Judit, the Dutch plumber, found out how wide when she went to the town hall with Spanish friends to seek support for an evening of the arts. 'Why,' they were asked, 'does Órgiva need an *Encuentra con cultura*? It has the half-marathon, what more does it need?'

Eventually they were granted a school room for their encounter with culture: a children's painting workshop, an evening of free entertainment including children's dancing, flamenco and performances by drama school students. They got the church too, after the bishop had vetted the programme of baroque music. Had someone thought they said rock? Church and school were packed, with people standing when seats ran out.

Baroque music was perfect for the eighteenth-century parish church. The musicians, with the golden retable for their backdrop, entranced us with a harpsichord and the sweet tones of a piccolo. They were professionals, German and Danish, who had settled in the Órgiva area. Usually they played to a handful of friends in a low-ceilinged house. To be given, and to fill, that beautiful church was a heady experience.

Part way through the concert, movement in the side aisle distracted us. Three Spanish women had come in, tourists taking in the monuments and architecture as though they had the place to themselves. Fascinated, we watched them reach the front pews. Now, surely, they must realize that what they were hearing was a live performance. Would they retreat? Would they stop and hear out the concert? Oh no, they wandered on, crossing themselves as they passed in front of the altar, which was also the point at which they passed between musicians and audience. The last we saw of them they were moving up the far aisle completing their circuit.

It was utterly impossible to imagine that scene taking place in Britain. A British trio would have died of embarrassment if they had blundered into a performance, they would have made themselves small and retreated. But the Spanish, we had read, do not understand the concept of self-consciousness. That evening we saw the point demonstrated.

Soon after, when La Taha announced a week of

127

culture, we doubted whether Albert and Sybella could again draw such a splendid audience for Monteverdi and Vivaldi. Fewer than a thousand people live there. The name encompasses seven white villages hanging on a slope above the deep channel of the river Trevélez. The church shared by Mecina, Fondales and Mecinilla made another fine concert hall, although the building had not fared well since it was sacked in the 1568 Moorish uprising. Reconstruction in the 1940s had left it bleak with only the restored woodwork of the roof to admire.

Once again there was no entrance fee, because these culture weeks were organized by town halls for their communities. Afterwards, drifting out into the night, we noticed men tying a white banner to the church wall. We vaguely wondered why, but there were a lot of people to talk to.

And one who did not want to speak to us. A woman we had eaten with the previous evening drove away. 'I suppose,' said Andrew, 'it was rather rude to tell her I thought playing golf in southern Spain was immoral.' Well, the conversation had become rather heated. After listening for ages to her telling us 'what is wrong with the Alpujarra' and that it 'needs a few golf courses', Andrew had forced some facts on her. Each day a single course used as much water as a town of 20,000 people or a family's supply for eight and a half years. We failed to understand how anyone could approve taking water from the mountains to squander on golf while people in towns had supplies cut. But it was true that golf brought high spending tourists and there were even rumours of plans to make the abandoned land into a course. These were soon followed by rumours of a three-star hotel too.

After the concert, the mayor and performers were first in the bar. The evening was declared a huge success and the mayor paid them more than the agreed fee. He had greater authority over things of that sort than his British counterpart. Pepe Jesús was an unusual Mayor. For a start, he spoke Japanese. He had lived in Japan and later helped bring a Japanese ballet shoe factory, which he managed, to his *pueblo*.

Altogether, the evening of the La Taha concert was memorable. We sat with friends outside the bar enjoying the cool evening air and the heavy scent of jasmine. At last we said our farewells and walked to the car. Suddenly we discovered the significance of the white banner. It was the screen for an outdoor film show. Pews were lined up in the square, facing the church wall. Our car was trapped the other side of a make-shift cinema and, worse, we had already seen *Kramer versus Kramer*.

The audience was largely made up of bemused children. Did the attitude to family life puzzle them? In Spain they benefited from a closeness and openness in family relations, and they were the centre of attention. Babies and toddlers were constantly stimulated, picked up, talked to and encouraged to look at this or that. After 'mama' and 'papa' the first word they seemed to learn was *mira*, look.

We were aware that crying or grizzling in a restaurant, bar, or shop, was invariably northern European. The Spanish had noticed too. One day Lesley and a friend were walking down an avenue in a park in a *costa* town when in the opposite direction came

129

a Spanish couple with a toddler. The boy, holding his parents' hands, was flopping, pretending his legs would not support him. His mother teased him: 'If you're not good we'll give you to the Englishwomen.'

'Whaaaa . . .' He had to be picked up and comforted, the threat was too awful.

The only bit of *Kramer versus Kramer* the La Taha children responded to was the nude scene which they found hilarious. Meanwhile, we were stuck. Lesley dozed in the passenger seat while Andrew watched the reel go round and round and was poised for a swift getaway the moment the interval came. Usually, the waiting came before an evening's enjoyment, not after. Our personal record was waiting two hours during Órgiva's encounter with culture. Where else, we wondered, would a hall full of people sit so patiently and good humouredly for that long, and without a bar in sight? Typically, no explanation was offered for the delay. We did not waste our time but successfully canvassed a home for two kittens, Columbus and a Lookalike. It meant letting them leave Cosmo at two months instead of three, but the new owner's children were impatient.

Eventually the concert began. Several different kinds of music, dancing and singing are traditional to Andalusia. Flamenco is two of them. There is the carnation in the hair, swirling polka-dot dress version that tourists see. Then there is the often mournful song and dance, that is said to come from deep in the soul. The music is a combination of guitar playing and hand-clapping, sometimes only clapping. Dancers are more likely to wear body-hugging Lycra and long black skirt than frilly dresses. Songs are frequently slow and sad *cante hondo*.

'Wobbly music', Lesley called it when we first heard it. We persevered watching performances on local television and in bars. Slowly it came to mean something, to express the sadness and gaiety that often walk together. Flamenco was, and is, gypsy music, but its origin is a mystery. The word dates from the last century but the music is believed by many to come from India. What is certain is that it expresses the hubris of a people who refuse to be down-trodden.

Yes, people do dance in the streets, but not flamenco. Other traditional dances are more fun and less hard on the feet. Miguel, at the bank, and his wife were accomplished dancers. We watched them outside a bar one fiesta night.

When we opened the bank account we had misgivings. A manual typewriter stood behind the counter, a signal that transactions would be time consuming. But no, a computer was hidden under the counter beside the ink pad for customers who signed with a thumb print. Ask and a statement was in your hand in seconds. Our misgivings were unfounded. Service was friendly, personal and efficient, with interest on our current account. Perhaps British bank managers should take to dancing in the streets.

There was plenty of home spun entertainment at the Alpujarra fiestas and Mari Carmen, our source of fresh vegetables and fiesta news, sent us off to see one of the more energetic ones, the annual re-enactment of a *Persianas y Cristianos* dust-up. Turbanned Moors clashed weapons with medieval Catholics; mock battle took place around a genuine Moorish fort; and the winning side marched through the main street of Velez Benaudalla to a band playing 'When the Saints Go Marching In'.

But we were also attracted by the international music festival at Granada. Ballet in the Generalife gardens perhaps? A concert in the palace of Charles V? Difficult, we were warned. Everyone had elaborate stories of failure to get tickets. Ours goes like this. We acquired a programme by dint of knocking on an unmarked door in the palace of Charles V, but the ticket office was not there. How could we find it? There were no clues in the programme and the man who handed it over was surprised to be asked. 'I don't know . . . yes, it's in the centre.' That was the best he could do.

'*Adelante*,' forward. 'The tourist office people will tell us.'

But they had closed for the fiesta. So had the town hall. People were dancing in the streets. In every square, they were dressed up and dancing, bands competing against each other for maximum volume. We abandoned all hope of booking seats for ballets and concerts, and stayed to watch. Great fun. Girls in flamenco dresses twirled and men strutted in Córdoban dress: striped trousers, short jackets and black stiff-brimmed hats. The whole city was swept away by music, and this was only early afternoon. A pity we could not stay until night.

CHAPTER SEVENTEEN

THE
STORM

SPRING WAS BECOMING summer. Wheat fields burned Andalusia gold. Greenery withered except on the well watered farms. Our neighbour Antonio had two pre-occupations – water and fire. Occasionally clouds relieved the blue: greyness spilled over the tops of the mountains into our valley. But rain seldom fell.

'Is there a chance of rain?' we would ask Antonio. Invariably he replied: 'Not until the new moon.'

Antonio was urging us to cut down the under-growth beneath our trees. Our Bermuda buttercups had been replaced by blue borage, two-coloured vetches and brilliant red poppies. While we under-stood his concern we liked our meadow. 'Let's enjoy our colourful carpet until we have to stop flood irrigation,' we decided. It would die down fast enough once we started directing water to individual trees.

Cosmo, meanwhile, was busy giving hunting lessons in our undergrowth. She demonstrated on imaginary prey, teaching the pair of Lookalikes and Isabella the not so gentle arts of stalking and pouncing. They resembled a family of miniature lions. We congratulated them on bringing us dead mice and chewed up lizards. 'Real *campo* cats,' Lesley said with the enthusiasm of the newly converted cat lover. 'They won't rely on packets of pet food, they'll feed themselves if they need to.' Next morning their offering was the savaged body of our nightingale. We could not accuse Posy. She had never hunted and by now she was an intermittent visitor to the house, although her injury was slowly healing.

Antonio raised the question again, diplomatically. 'Are you going to cut back the plants?' Translated it meant: 'Foreigners don't understand the danger.'

'Soon, soon,' we replied, meaning *mañana, mañana*.

We recognized the danger. Scorched trees on the edge of the abandoned land were a constant reminder. The previous summer the abandoned land had burned. Until then its open field, cropped short by sheep and goats, had been luxuriant. The story of the big fire had entered the folklore along with the one about the deluge. Olive trees burst into flames before the fire reached them, so intense was the heat. Local radio appealed for help, particularly from those with chainsaws, to cut a fire break. A plane scooped sea water and raced inland to drop it. Hundreds of people fought the blaze, fought desperately because it could so easily have encircled the town.

134

Fears were well-founded: they remembered the horror of the fire a dozen years earlier when forest covering the Lújar burned. From our house we looked across to the Lújar and measured the slow regenerative growth of gorse and pine.

Then the television began showing film of reservoirs only one-third full, and forest fires. Persuaded, we cut down our flowers. Francis, who also had a Muslim name, came to do it with his heavy-duty strimmer. He was clearing ground near the pool when Andrew went to offer him tea.

'His back was to me and I thought he was having a pee,' Andrew said afterwards. 'How was I to know he was praying? You don't immediately think, Ah! he's facing east, he must be praying.'

Francis was part of the cosmopolitan community of Muslims, converts to the Sufi sect, in the Granada area. Apparently they chose it for the resonances of Spain's Moorish period, an unsatisfactory explanation considering they could have settled in an Islamic country. It was, though, the only one on offer.

Sad to lose the flowers from our orchard, we realized the importance of reassuring our neighbours. Our first bonfire of olive cuttings had given us an idea of how fire behaved in a dry climate. Green leaves fizzed like fireworks, wisps of grass were fuses carrying flames. It was trying to spread like ... well ... wildfire.

When the Lújar burned the smell permeated the whole valley. People in the high villages sat on their balconies watching the distant fire and feeling the hot dry wind it generated. Some claimed that the loss of the forest had altered the climate, making it drier.

By comparison the fire on the abandoned land had been inconsequential. That year an area of Spain one and half times the size of greater London had been devastated. Damage was estimated at more than £400 million, but the environmental damage was incalculable. Even so, vigilance was having some effect. During our time in Spain, the number of fires rose, perhaps due to better record keeping, but the burned area decreased by three-fifths and the financial cost by two-thirds.

One evening we saw for ourselves the speed of a mountain fire fanned by breeze. Looking up from our patio table we noticed a red glow behind the shoulder of the Lújar. Immediately a bright red line was running across the ridge. Fire rounded the mountain three miles from us and flames shot up. Firefighters' vehicles flashed through the dusk. A plane was used and the fire contained but not before dozens of acres of young trees were destroyed.

Firewatchers have only eagles and the lost for company. That was how we met one of the men whose job it is to scan the landscape for smoke. We had taken a wrong turning and ran out of dirt road at the top of a 400 foot cliff. Above us was a hut where we found the firewatcher whitewashing his summer home – a cabin with fireplace, bed, cooker and plenty of radio equipment. He lived on the roof of the world. Mountain ranges and blue sea stretched away below him. He drew us a map and, reluctantly, we went away.

We thought of him months later when a village rubbish tip was set alight. No danger, but within ten minutes a helicopter was overhead checking. When a summer ban on agricultural and garden fires was introduced it seemed a sensible precaution against unnecessary call-outs.

Our 50,000 litre swimming pool was supposed to be our water supply for emergencies. So when José said he was ready to test his repairs we were relieved. There would be more work later, he said, but that would not stop us swimming. He had to completely fill the enormous pool because the last litre might prove too much and open a crack. A hose was rigged up. The water began to trickle in. He guessed it would take a week, but it took ten days.

Sharing water between the pool and the house, there was not enough pressure to operate the washing machine. Then the machine packed up altogether, unable to pump out. Andrew investigated. Jammed in the pump was the key to the motorbike dumped by our hedge.

Rain came, as Antonio had predicted, with the change in the moon. The sky over the sea looked bruised, then darkness spread. The first clouds came as wisps across the waning moon. To begin with the wind was a gentle ripple in the olive leaves. But it was the start of a tempest from Africa.

The noise of the wind among the trees rose. Drops fell, water stained the colour of the Sahara. We secured shutters, stuffed rugs at the bottom of doors. Nothing could keep out the wind. It thrashed rain, whipped branches. The noise was tiring, like sitting in a station waiting room as a never-ending express roared through. The wind threw smoke back down the chimneys at us. There was no comfort.

'Cosmo and the kittens. We can't leave them out in this. The tea chest will blow away.' With the kittens indoors and feeding contentedly, our thoughts turned to James and Elena.

'They've chosen their life. After all, they have a caravan to go to.'

In the morning, as we surveyed fallen branches and other ravages of the storm, we wished we had asked them in. Instead we had slept in a house with three empty bedrooms. We had treated cats more kindly than two human beings.

Books on etiquette do not tell you how to approach people you have left out in a storm. Andrew found them folding their plastic sheet. Three times in the night it had blown down. He opted for the imperative: 'Come and have coffee.' In the kitchen they drank coffee and ate biscuits like conventional neighbours dropping in. No reproach, but a thank you for the coffee. We felt even worse.

Fortunately they had decided to move on to a nice dry cave in Sacramonte, the old gypsy quarter of Granada. They planned to busk in the city. We gave them a lift as far as Lanjarón where we were going to replace gas bottles. Shamed, we left them hitch hiking out of our lives.

The day came when we felt confident we could tell José his repair had worked. But Antonio was waiting for us by his gate as we came down the mule track. 'The German man working on the pool, he's dead.'

Too shocking to believe. Then: 'How?'

'An accident in Tablones, across the river. A machine broke.' Antonio gestured a cut across his chest.

We clutched at the idea that Antonio had been told a false rumour. There were always plenty of those. Or perhaps we had misunderstood him. Maybe José had been injured. In town though his death was confirmed. The blade of the cutting machine he had warned Lesley against had shattered, slicing through his chest, killing him within seconds.

The funeral was at the cemetery overlooking the town, a typical Andalusian columbarium with white walls and cypress trees. In the chapel there was room only for the priest, immediate family and José's neighbour. The *Guardia* had gone to her to identify the body, and all the rest had fallen to her too. She had told us some of it.

'The undertakers brought a coffin but it was so ornate I said he wouldn't want that. Then they fetched this one and put him in it with his working boots on. I told them: "He's not going to be buried in his working boots." '

The crowd gathered outside the chapel parted to allow pall bearers to carry the coffin out. Two workmen waited on a scaffold to receive it and guide it into a slot in the wall. Someone handed up a key to the gates of heaven. One of the workmen placed it on top of the coffin. Then they built a wall. José would, no doubt, have said the workmanship was not up to German standards.

Over the months he had struggled with our pool we had grown to like him and the little dog who always accompanied him. When he was not building, he organized paragliding holidays and we often watched his clients floating down 6,500 feet to the abandoned land. At first glance they were eagles, but gradually the reds, yellows and greens of parachutes emerged from the blue. Then we made out the flyers.

Eventually they swooped over the house aiming for the recovery party at the bar near the bridge. José had found something of the freedom he wanted in the Alpujarra. A sun-warmed tomb, with eagles flying above, seemed right for him.

CHAPTER EIGHTEEN

INTERLUDE

WE WENT AWAY, for a day or two.

A fast road took us west, into vast rolling sierras. We drove through golden miles of sunflowers beneath skies of shining blue. The colours were pure and true. This was another Andalusia, the one where there is nobody in the countryside, where buildings cluster in villages, where a single farm stretches further than you can see; and where they grow sunflowers for oil.

The journey stays in the mind, more vivid than the hilltop towns, crowned with castles and convents, where we paused. More precious than the proud city where we took a dutiful look at flowery patios.

Then we were home again. Grey water, a mix of irrigation water and sewage, was swilling along the channels towards our land. We quickened our steps, ready to deal with an inundation. But before we reached the house we realized it was Antonio's field behind our house which was being irrigated, not our land.

Lesley ran down the slope at the end of the mule track calling to cats and kittens. Cosmo and the two Lookalikes frisked around her. Posy glided grandly, as if it did not matter to her whether we had returned or not, but when Andrew took the food box from by the washing machine, where we had left it for the friend who fed the cats in our absence, Posy was first at the bowl.

'Where's Isabella?' Lesley went in search of the tortoiseshell.

'Stuck up a tree?' Andrew suggested. He walked around the garden, listening for kittenish woe. Privately, he thought she might have been killed by a dog. On and off through the evening we hunted, but Lesley guessed from the first she had been stolen. The motorbike had also gone from its place by the hedge.

Next morning foul water was still flooding Antonio's field and seeping from the bank against which our house was built. Rooms stank of decay.

The house by the river had never been an easy house. We had fought off invasions of earwigs, ants, fruit flies, beetles and cockroaches. Mice had nested in a spare bed. During Lesley's mother's visit a vividly marked snake had appeared on a fluffy white rug: a viper, although none of us had admitted then that we knew what it was. And now we found we could not go away without nailing down the cat.

We decided to move.

142

CHAPTER NINETEEN

HOUSEHUNTING

'IF WE LIVED in the town we'd be able to have *chocolate con churros* for breakfast.' That was one of our considerations when we started househunting again. Like the Spanish, we enjoy walking out in the evenings to meet friends and perhaps take a drink with them and in the mornings we like hot crusty bread and the day's newspaper. Although we love the country we are essentially urban dwellers.

We pictured ourselves breakfasting on rich drinking chocolate, dipping into it the crisply browned batter of the *churros*. Spain's favourite breakfast is Lesley's too. The chocolate is thick as custard. Expedient Spanish clergy had ruled it a drink; therefore it did not break the fast and could be taken before Mass. It became enormously popular. 'It is made,' wrote

Richard Ford 150 years ago, 'just liquid enough to come within the benefit of clergy, that is a spoon will almost stand up in it.'

Churros from the *churrería* in Órgiva were as good as any we had tasted. The worn wooden door opened into a white painted room with a vat of hot oil. As with a good chip shop in England, you had to wait while the next batch was cooked. Batter was swirled from a funnel into boiling oil. All eyes watched the tightly coiled snake darken to chestnut brown, as though, despite having seen the transformation many times, they doubted that the runny flour and water paste could turn into *churros*. The cook prodded the batter with giant tongs. When she judged it cooked, she lifted it out on to the counter to be snipped with scissors into eight inch lengths, then bundled up in squares of paper. Anticipation sharpens appetite and it is impossible to get home without chewing a piece. By moving into town we would be able to enjoy that as often as we liked.

Javier told us about a flat. 'On the top floor of the block near the market. It has a swimming pool.' Well, that was different. Top flats had superb views, and a rooftop pool had a ring of penthouse glamour. 'But it's unfurnished,' he added, and ended our penthouse dream.

Órgiva does not have estate agents with shop windows, it is a word of mouth business practised by a few people as a sideline to their normal work. Javier was an odd-job man who looked after a large house and garden. As we walked up the street together he pointed out a 'very nice' flat. It was above a disco. We walked on. The next one was in a quiet street, but the owner was not there to meet us. So we drove a short distance out of town to a modern house on the main road. It belonged, he said, to a judge. The neighbour who was expected to have the key did not. Apparently the judge was a nervous man: his house was protected by the toughest window bars and iron gates we had seen. This was daunting, but what put us off entirely was the stone yard next door. We had to speak above the sound of saws whining their way through marble.

Javier had other properties in town to show us, or not show us, but they had to wait for another evening. A friend of a friend had arranged for us to see over a house in one of the villages of the Poqueira valley that joins the Guadalfeo near Órgiva. When we had looked for houses before coming to Spain we had viewed some up there. The snag was that if they were modernized their owners demanded the high rates short-term holiday-makers paid.

Turning into the Poqueira valley we saw the familiar sight of Pampaneira, Bubión and Capileira, like white splashes on the hillside. Our road was fairly level, the valley floor rising to meet us, but once we reached the hydro-electric station below Pampaneira, we started on the hairpin bends. We could see the road high above, below it a sheer cliff falling to the river. Terrifying the first time we had driven it, familiarity had made it less nerve-wracking than rush hour on London's Embankment. Within living memory there had been nothing more than a mule track up the valley, and villages of the High Alpujarra had been amongst the most isolated in Spain.

Pampaneira, the lowest of the Poqueira villages,

was on the principal road and therefore easily accessible to coaches on day trips from the coast or Granada. Capileira, the highest, was the starting point for mountain walks. Above it was Spain's highest road which, when the snow has melted, takes adventurous drivers to Granada. Bubión, where we were heading, had become the home of artists and crafts people from the rest of Spain and northern Europe.

Conchita looked after the house we were to see. She lived at the top of a precipitous street, near the village wash house, an open sided low-roofed structure with two rows of sinks. Although people own washing machines they keep one of these sinks on the roof or in the yard for especially dirty jobs. Deep and square, they have a ridged cement washing board. Conchita was one of the last women in Bubión to take her washing to the wash house. Another survival was the family which was the last to keep goats on the lower floor of their house. Bubión had been gentrified.

Despite her name, Conchita had none of the fragility of a little shell. She sped us up a slippery cobbled street and into a cul de sac, past a bar with tables and chairs stacked outside. The house we were going to see blocked the end of the street; its typical first floor balcony had been glazed to provide extra room. Conchita said: 'An artist worked there. Wouldn't it also be good for a writer?' She pointed below the balcony. 'You can park the car here.'

'What about the bar?' Obviously, the tables and chairs were set out in the street.

'They'll move them when you want to get in or out.'

Inside, the house was hard, cool, clean, white

painted and dark. A typical village house. Furniture was sparse: upright chairs, a round wooden table, the ubiquitous *mesa camilla* with *brasero* below. Except for the electric light bulbs hanging from the centre of each ceiling and the bottled gas and stove in the kitchen, Richard Ford's description would have served. Each room was, he wrote, whitewashed and 'thus scrupulously clean and free from insects. The furniture is scanty, for much would harbour vermin and caloric [heat]; coolness and space are the things wanting.' Some rooms lacked windows, not unusual where houses were built on top of and around each other as though put together by a child toying with Lego.

Next day Javier offered modern flats in the town. Again, there was a total lack of colour except in the Sacred Heart above the matrimonial bed. Javier explained that furnished housing was not easy to find in Órgiva because people came to work in banks and other offices for fairly short periods. We were not the only people wanting new keys.

'*Chaves danos los llaves*' – Chaves, give us the keys – said the placards held by students demonstrating outside the town hall. Chaves was the prime minister of Andalusia but what keys was he withholding and why? Mari Carmen had the answer when we bought our tomatoes. 'The students want the keys to the new school. They're still having to make do with the old school while the new one stands empty.'

'But why can't they move?'

'Well, the contractor hasn't been paid and he won't hand over the keys until he's got the money.'

'The government must have known it would have to pay.'

147

'Oh, yes,' she smiled.

Our househunting continued. One property had been mentioned several times. It belonged to a woman who had moved to the coast but it was unclear whether she was selling or letting. When we telephoned her she was going abroad but was willing to let and asked a friend to show us round.

Her house was large, modern and stripped of furniture. No furniture, no good. As we came out, the woman who had shown us round introduced us to neighbours talking in the street. One of them, a Danish man with a vigorous Alsatian dog, said: 'So what you two are looking for is a comfortable house with a couple of bedrooms and a swimming pool about six kilometres from the town.'

'Oh, if only we could find such a place!' said Lesley.

'It is mine. You can have it,' he said.

And we arranged to look at Las Monjas the following day.

LAS MONJAS was the colour of the earth, built of rough stone. It sat on a hillside, looking down the valley and out to the sea. Turn and you saw the snow on the peaks. 'It is,' said Lesley, 'the best view in the world.'

We had followed Ole up six kilometres of bends to Carataunas and then down a neck-breaking dirt track, blocked by an old fridge which we had to shift. That was our main reservation – Las Monjas lay below a rubbish tip. Our other doubt was the quirky water supply.

'There might be somewhere better,' we said. But we did not seriously believe that. Having opted for one romantic dream we were being cautious. The narrow

148

terraces of Las Monjas, scrawny from neglect, could be made into a beautiful garden. We pictured walks with a *mirador* – viewing point – here and a fountain there, under the shade of a vine. Although we wanted to be practical, it was a house that encouraged dreams. And we knew other houses where dreams were coming true.

Albert and Paul had made their garden on an equally steep slope. We went there to hear Albert play on a piano they had carried down to their house 300 feet below the road. Other friends, Lynda and Lars, insisted we meet them on the road because we might not find the house unaided. Together the four of us plunged down into a narrow valley, facing a sheer cliff. We negotiated barking dogs tugging at chains. We slipped on mud. Then suddenly we were strolling along a terrace overhung with purple bougainvillea.

Past clumps of black and green bamboo, it widened to a *mirador* with roses and rock plants growing by a low wall. Over the edge was an oval of bright green grass, surrounded by shrubs and trees. 'We have plenty of water from springs and the *acequia*,' said Paul, who is the gardener, suggesting his work had played no part in it.

He led us through a series of gardens, past first lilies, then peonies, and in the distance a bright splash of poppies. A pool, like an over-sized hip bath built into the slope, provided a place to cool off when the heat became intolerable. Paul named plants that we, poor gardeners, could not. But we recognized ground elder. 'A mistake,' he admitted. An aunt had promised periwinkle for ground cover but without its blue flowers she had been confused.

We walked back to the house, the air filled with the scent of jasmine that clung to its walls. And when we sat drinking *costa*, the deep pink local wine, Albert told with his dry humour of early morning visitors to the garden.

'I opened my eyes and there, outside the window, were two *Guardia*. "Oh my God!" I thought. "Whatever it is I don't care," and I closed my eyes and pretended to be asleep. I got up two hours later and they'd gone. Consuela, our neighbour above, was furious. They'd taken her plants.'

Someone else cut in: 'She wasn't growing pot!'

'No.' Albert giggled. 'They took her African marigolds. Pulled them up and put them in plastic evidence bags. They came back the next day with some very bedraggled marigolds and an apology.'

The creation of gardens is a venerable tradition in Andalusia. In the thirteenth century, Ibn Luyun, a poet from Almeria, described the ideal country house.

'Select a dominant place to construct a house and garden, to keep watch and defend it well.

'It should face the noon sun, and the fountain or pool should be slightly raised, or better, in place of the fountain there should be a water channel running under the shade of trees and plants.

'Close-by, beds will be planted with evergreens of many kinds to brighten the view and further off flowers of all types and evergreen trees.

'The house will be surrounded by vines and in the central part it will be shaded by trellises covering the walks and flanking the paths that run along the borders on one side. In the centre an open pavilion will be installed for the house of rest, framed by climbing rose trees, myrtle and all manner of beautiful garden flowers.

'It will be longer than it is broad so that the eye will not tire in its contemplation.

'A pavilion will be set aside in the lower part for guests who come to bear company to its master. It will have its own door and pool which, hidden by a clump of trees, will not be seen from afar. It will be fitting also to build a dovecote and an habitable tower.'

Without knowing the quotation, David and Dorothy had arrived at something close to Ibn Luyun's prescription. The house David designed stands on an eminence of dry land above the olive groves. They built it with thick walls like a castle and above the bulk rises the tower of David's studio with windows to the east, west and north. Close to the house Dorothy has created vine covered walkways and planted acacia, rose, myrtle, quince, tuberose, barberry, and blue iris beloved of the Moors.

The house looks down on a line of three ponds, a dovecote, and beyond them the guest house or *casita*. Everywhere there are the young trees she has planted: olives, mulberry, eucalyptus ... The swimming pool is an irregular bowl surrounded by oleander, its shower a Greek pillar that spouts water.

The approach to the house is through a great olive grove, where hoopoes pass the summer. When the olive grove gives way to *secano*, dry land, dotted with shrubs of rosemary, the house rises up ahead of you.

The entrance is a wooden door into a walled patio with raised flower beds and a lion-headed fountain on a wall. Passing through the house, its beamed ceiling supported by the worn wooden screw of an olive press, you come to the garden, the eye travelling beyond to the encircling mountains.

Knowing Dorothy to be an inordinate animal lover, we called round before moving house to ask whether she could cope with another kitten. But her total of cats had recently jumped to nine and she had also taken in a stray dog. There were the doves too . . .

CHAPTER TWENTY

THE HOUSE
ON THE HILL

YES, WE TOLD OLE, we would like to rent Las Monjas, the house on the hill. As he gave us the keys, he told us sadly: 'It is the house where my happy memories are.' He made us feel a responsibility to like it, but we already sensed that we would. Once, when we had been buying a house in England, a surveyor said to us: 'This may not seem a professional thing to say, but I always go by the feel of a house. If I were you, I'd buy this one. It feels right.'

Our list of the pros and cons of Las Monjas was definitely longer on the debit side but it felt right. On the credit side was an excellent room for Lesley to work; arm chairs; a drive right up to the house; and sublime views. Against, was the rubbish tip but you could not actually see that. Although the track was treacherous, our jeep could cope. The insects boring through the beams sounded as loud as rabbits but we were persuaded their active season was coming to an end. The spring that supplied water might run dry but had not done so in the past. We found a 'but' to counteract all the disadvantages because we had decided before we made the list.

House and setting were quite different from our first house but no less beautiful. Wild freesias grew there, along with cistus, thyme and rusty foxgloves. Gorse splashed the terraces with gold, borage flashed deep blue. Because our water tank was cracked a bank behind the house was lush with shrubs, ferns and mint. Attracted by the seeping water, birds fussed there all day. Blue butterflies danced among the silver-green olive trees. The sea was not always a blue and distant blur. Some days it was stitched with threads of gold, the horizon a fine gold line, as sunlight pierced a bank of cloud. At Las Monjas we had skyscapes as well as landscapes, and nights of shooting stars.

Ole had designed the house himself in the 1970s and had it built by a local builder. Lesley wrote to a friend: 'If you visit pack a pair of flares because it's like walking into a seventies time warp.' Furniture, tiles, and plastic flat-pack lampshades designed by Ole, were all of the period.

Las Monjas had an irregularly shaped living-room with a kitchen at one end, a dining-room, which became Lesley's study as we ate outside, and two bedrooms. The windows had the traditional *rejas*, iron grilles, which once served to keep young lovers apart in long nights of courtship. Now they brought a rebate

154

on our insurance and allowed us to leave windows open when we went out.

The inside needed a coat of whitewash as walls were streaked where rain had come through the *launa*. The land was overgrown and dry, but all it needed was irrigation. Water pipes and kitchen taps were encrusted with lime-scale. Things like that were only to be expected in a house unoccupied for a year. Floors were dusty with sawdust where giant woodworm had escaped from chestnut beams supporting the stone slabs of the roof. But the house smelled fresh and airy and dry.

Ole came up to help us get the water heater working. As they worked together on the water supply Andrew commented on the shower head similar to one we owned. It was another of Ole's simple and effective ideas. He liked to talk about his life, how as a young engineer he had emigrated to Brazil and saved up to send the boat fare to the woman who was to be his wife. He started his own business making a self-lubricating bearing he had invented. Then there were the years in Denmark, numerous inventions, and finally the move to Spain. For a while he and his family were happy at Las Monjas. Then came the awful tragedy: the deaths of his wife and a daughter in her twenties.

Before moving in, we went back to the hypermarkets of Granada to buy some things for our new house – metal-framed director chairs (as insects had destroyed the traditional straw-seated ones) and chemicals for the pool. And then we headed to the Albaicín. One day, for a mad half-hour, we had thought we might live in a *carmen*. An English couple

155

were giving up the house they rented and a friend asked: 'Wouldn't you like it?' But a telephone call later we knew it was in urgent need of repairs and not to be relet. A pity, a *carmen* in the Albaicín is a smart address.

Carmens are houses with enclosed gardens. The Moors built them originally – as the suburban villas of their time – and the style has continued. The Albaicín is a maze of steep streets looking across to the Alhambra and beyond it the Sierra. Next to the Albaicín is the Sacramonte, where the gypsies used to live in caves. Nowadays they commute to them from their flats in town to put on flamenco shows for tourists.

We wondered whether James and Elena had found an empty cave. And what was the correct behaviour if you met a busker you knew? Walk by, pretending you did not know them? Drop a coin in the hat? Or greet them as old friends? We could not decide.

Next day we got down to work sprucing up Las Monjas. We bought a bag of whitewash, called *cal*, a bucket and brushes. The brushes are round, three inches in diameter with long, soft bristles. Paint was available but *cal* has its advantages. It is cheaper, and the lime deters insects. The Spanish talk about 'cleaning' with *cal* and it is really a part of the spring cleaning.

In the villages whitewashing is women's work. They form co-operative teams and work intensely freshening houses inside and out. We noticed that most painting is done by women, including the yellow lines in the plaza which were the prelude to another attempt to control parking. But we worked together and quickly realized the first skill to be mastered was mixing powder and water to the right consistency. Too thin and it did not stay on the brush; too thick and it set like plaster, impossible to spread. Whitewash splashes more than paint but it is also easier to remove. In a couple of days we had painted and cleared up. The house appeared clean and fresh. We sat down and switched on the television. Arabic, from Morocco. We added a new aerial to our shopping list.

The house was named after the well: Las Monjas, the well of the nuns. Its water had once been celebrated as a cure for eye ailments, but one look in the tank deterred us from either drinking it or putting it on our eyes. All the time we lived there, we collected drinking water from one or other of the roadside springs.

There was a fine spring on the road to Órgiva but it was not our favourite. Whenever we went to Lanjarón, the town where we bought bottles of gas for our cooker, we filled our twenty-five-litre plastic container at the Spring of the Oleander. The mineral water of Lanjarón is among the most famous in Spain, bottled and sold throughout the country. For us it was free.

Even better, we could go in another direction and fill up with naturally sparkling water. A reaction with lime brought this fizzy water to the surface in a spring surrounded by chestnut trees. It tasted similar to Badoit water but only once did we fill our big container and stagger the half mile to the car. Afterwards we limited ourselves to five-litre bottles.

We settled in very happily at the house of the happy memories. From its narrow terraces of olive and orange trees, we walked out on to the dry lands, a natural rock garden filled with thyme, rosemary and aromatic herbs unfamiliar to us. Scent rose at every step. We continued to give Rafael lifts to and from town. Oh yes, he understood the pleasure we took in the dry lands. 'Who passes rosemary and does not pick it does not have loves, nor plans to have them,' he recited. So we picked rosemary and put a sprig in a narrow stemmed vase by our fireplace.

All we now lacked were bookcases and even the most basic ones in the hypermarkets were expensive. The answer was *machihembrados*, earthenware planks a metre long and twenty centimetres deep and perhaps three centimetres thick. They are traditionally used with bricks and cement to build everything from shelves to kitchen units. In most places where a northern European would use wood, the Andalusian uses *machihembrados*, which literally translates as male/female, for they are made to fit together with one edge convex and the other concave. Some friends used them to build kitchen units but did not fix them and tile until they had lived with the kitchen for months and were certain everything was in the right place. Our shelves were not fixed either but they looked good, the red terracotta against the white walls.

When we moved in we agreed to take a guest, Bertie, a cat belonging to a couple who were going to Scotland to be married. By now we were regarded as expert cat carers. Cosmo, the remaining pair of Lookalikes and the intermittent Posy were all dispatched to new homes when Sally, their owner, arrived on holiday at the house just after we moved out. We did not see any of them again.

Bertie was a four month old tabby, with a coat as silky as Cosmo's but lacking her ear tufts. On his first day he learned it was a mistake to pounce on cactus but he never learned it was futile to chase geckos.

We had geckos, less sleek and with larger heads than other lizards, in each room: big ones about five inches long, baby ones, and some who were regrowing lost tails. They crept out from stone ceilings and posed on walls until, with a flashing movement, they caught unwary insects. Bertie flashed too but they were too quick for him, running up walls and across ceilings, suspended by the microscopic hooks on their toes.

In some villages they are abhorred as much as mice or snakes and thought venomous, in others regarded as lucky. We enjoyed them, from their deep clack-clack-clack calls to their fat little fingers. Sitting outside over supper we watched them on a pillar gobbling up insects drawn by lamplight and disputing the richest territory. On the evenings we did not sit out we put the lamp on anyway. Feeding the geckos, we called it.

Other uninvited guests were less fun although there was nothing, except a jumping spider, that alarmed us. We were visited by huge black bees that bumbled into us but never thought of stinging; ants from half an inch long to minute; wasps that did not sting and house flies that did; a praying mantis; lizards; small snakes and big ones; the occasional tick; big black beetles; swallow tail butterflies; sand flies so tiny they slipped through fly screens; cicadas; and always crunching in the beams those wretched long horned beetles, *capricornios*.

In hot weather flies were such a nuisance that it made sense not to eat before sundown when they automatically disappeared. We tried flypapers which they avoided; sprays that threatened to choke us too; and an ultra violet lamp, the kind used in food shops. They liked the lamp best. They settled on it so we knew where to find them and swat them.

Bedevilled by flies, one friend sought advice on pest control from the Ministry of Agriculture in England. The expert listened to his problem, then said: 'Well, what I do is I take a newspaper, I roll it up and . . .'

CHAPTER TWENTY-ONE

ON THE
TWELFTH DAY OF
THE DULA

CARATAUNAS means tranquil place. True, not a lot happens there. But you would not expect much in the smallest municipality in one of the remotest regions of Spain. Our village has all the trappings of a town, a mayor and town hall, but only 175 inhabitants.

The village lies secreted away behind the curve of the hill. Unless you live in Carataunas, there is no reason to take the short side road to its centre. But many people stop at the junction because it has been widened to make a lay-by and view point. They probably did not know they were at Carataunas, until the council put up a ceramic sign, made by Diego, our potter. Diego was a master of glazes and produced a landscape in tiles, showing the mountains all the way down to the Mediterranean. It was impressionistic, but then so was the view. Colours changed, distances altered and mountains blended into mountains. In certain light it seemed one mountain was transparent and you could see through it to the next.

We seldom went into the village because our track dropped down behind the first building you came to, the bar. It was not a bar as most people understand the word. Not even a room, only outside tables where you could sit and drink beer or *costa* and eat tapas. But all the village used our track. Fifty yards along there was a railing with an oil drum set into it to make a chute. And fifty feet below the chute was a bowl shape scooped out of the hillside. This served as a rubbish tip. The track went through three extraordinarily tight hairpin bends before arriving at Las Monjas. When we walked to the village we avoided the tip by taking a mule track from the first hairpin above the house. Lesley swore it was vertical. Beautiful too, it was shadowed by fig trees until it emerged in the heart of the village.

We went up first to buy bread and wine and enquire about claiming our irrigation water. You would not find the shop if you did not know it was there, but we had been told to go to a door to the left of some grey gates and ring the bell. A voice called down from the first floor: 'Who's there?'

'I'm Andrés.' No one in the village knew us, but we assumed they had heard of us, maybe watched our car inclining down the track.

'What do you want?'

'I want to buy some things.'

'Wait a moment.'

A neat, grey haired woman came and opened the

grey gates. We followed her into a great barn of a room, the centre of which was empty. At the back were piles of crates and sacks and to the right a counter in front of shelves. The woman stepped behind the counter and took the pose of a shopkeeper. After introductions – she was Isabella – Andrew asked: 'Do you have bread?'

'No, but a baker calls. I can get bread for you and you can collect it later.'

'Good. Just one loaf.' We bought pasta, wine, cheese and pies filled with angel hair jam made from the flesh of a squash, a popular filling for pastries. Then we asked about irrigation water. 'Who should we see? We are supposed to get it on the twelfth day of the *dula*.'

She crossed to the far side of the great barn and called upstairs. A young man, her son, came down. She asked him if we were right about the twelfth day of the *dula*.

'That would be it,' he said.

'But when,' Andrew persisted, 'is the twelfth day of the *dula*?' Ole had mentioned that the village had not got to grips with the Julian calendar and clung to the Moorish system for water rights.

Isabella and her son set about complicated calculations involving a wall calendar. The information was there if one knew how to extract it, as the *dula* is the length of half a moon. 'Yesterday!' they cried in unison. So we had missed our water for another two weeks.

Our land had been untended for years and the dying orange trees and unpruned olives were chronically short of water. Brambles thrived. We calculated

163

how to eke out our water, between house and land. The spring provided enough for some of the watering but we decided that would be best used on the lower terraces via the swimming pool.

Behind the house there was a storage pond, one which could be fed from either the spring or the irrigation channels. Despite energetic and backbreaking work, our efforts to clear it and bring it into use again failed. So did our attempts to take our irrigation water, because the channels on our neighbour's land above us were broken. Walls of terraces had collapsed into the *acequia* and dumped building material blocked the water course. The twelfth day of the *dula* came and went without a drop of *acequia* water coming our way.

In truth the land was returning to the mountain, as was much of the area. These terraces had not been profitable and now there were not enough people to work them anyway, barely a third of the number there had been thirty years earlier in Carataunas. Not long ago our mountainside had been filled with the sounds of *azadones* breaking the soil, and women talking at the well. People had lived in a hamlet fifty yards below Las Monjas. By the time we moved there, the hamlet had been abandoned to yellow broom and pink oleander.

We heard several versions of the 'real' history of the hamlet, but what was plainly correct was that during the 1970s houses were sold as holiday homes by a Scandinavian company. A handful remained habitable, and were used for a week or two each year, but the rest were derelict. Gaping windows revealed squatters' rubbish and the vandalized bathrooms installed in the seventies. Several houses had never been modernized. Their roofs had fallen in, beams leaning against fireplaces.

Lizards lazed on the ruin of its cobbled street, and goats foraged for anything that grew between the stones. The vehicle track ended a few yards below our entrance, at the top of the hamlet. From there, down into the valley of the river Chico, was only a mule track. It ran beside *acequias*, beneath shady olive trees and by fields where brown cows browsed. It passed abandoned farms, crossed the dry bed of the Chico and arrived at the village of Bayacas.

Land on the floor of the Chico valley was cultivated, the fields won from rocky ground, their earth retained by stone walls. The path between Bayacas and Carataunas was regularly used. Every day a farmer carried milk churns from the valley up to Carataunas. Occasionally a man called to ask if we had seen a straying mule, but these conversations were tricky because there is a whole vocabulary of description for animals and we did not know it. Most of the users were hikers or holidaymakers on horseback. In summer their hands were stained red from picking mulberries, a reminder of when silk was made here.

Perhaps the Granada poet Federico García Lorca walked this path one Christmas in the 1920s, when he and the composer Manuel de Falla stayed at the Cortijo del Montijano, home of Rafael Aguado. He certainly went to Carataunas: he wrote to his brother that while he was in the village he heard about the *Guardia* beating up some gypsies there.

And it was while staying at Bayacas with Aguado whose house, like ours, looked down to the river

Chico, that he heard a local ballad which led him to write 'The Unfaithful Wife'. It begins:

So I took her to the river
Thinking she was a virgin,
But she had a husband.

On the poet's birthday we went to Fuente Vaqueros, where he was born, in Granada's *Vega*. We were promised a celebration *a las cinco de la tarde, en punto*, at five in the afternoon, exactly. A stage and sound system were being set up in the square, but the Lorca house-museum was shut. 'It's closed for the birthday celebrations,' we were told in a shop with a sign promising tourist information. We relayed the news to other nonplussed English speakers who were quartering the town. We gave it one more try, and hammered on the museum door. A head popped out. 'We're closed.'

'But what about the readings promised for five in the afternoon?'

'Oh, yes, come back at eight-thirty.' We were given invitation cards.

There was nothing to do except go to a bar. There was bullfighting on the television, appropriate as *A las cinco de la tarde* is the first line of Lorca's eulogy for his *matador* friend Ignacio Sanchez Mejias. The bull in the televised fight declined to take part and the president draped a green handkerchief over the front of the box. 'What,' we asked a farmer beside us in the bar, 'does that signify?'

'He's giving permission for the bull to be withdrawn and replaced by another.'

Nothing was going smoothly that evening, not even the *corrida*.

By eight-thirty we were once again standing outside the museum, a mixed crowd of Spanish and foreigners who had breached the museum's defences and acquired invitations. Posh cars arrived and the passengers were allowed in. We waited. At 9.07 exactly the door opened and the hoi polloi were beckoned in.

Upstairs was a committee of people, the more elderly seated. No one bothered to introduce anyone, we were left to assume from the details on the invitation that those sitting were survivors from La Barraca, the travelling theatre company founded by Lorca and friends. A large and familiar-looking man in a patchwork jacket made a brief speech in awkward Spanish. 'Who's that?' people around us muttered, and in the end someone asked him. He was Yevgeny Yevtushenko, who later talked to Lesley about the novel he was writing and his search for a London publisher.

How strange chance meetings can be! Yevtushenko recorded one in his poem 'Encounter' about a man in an airport bar.

It was the very image of Hemingway.
(Later I heard that it was Hemingway.)

One thing Lorca and Hemingway shared was a love of bullfighting. And also, it seemed, the admiration of a Russian poet.

We were handed glasses of wine and soon after shooed out into the street, the women clutching single red roses. A rock band was deafening the place.

When Lorca visited Carataunas, in the mid-1920s,

he may have paused at the Las Monjas spring. One of our olive trees overhung the track and in our time there was a wall where passers-by invariably rested. But in any case that stretch was a natural place to pause and look down on the view. Occasionally we discovered people seeking the well which they had heard of as a cure for tired and sore eyes. We had to disappoint them: it was only accessible by lifting a heavy stone slab, below which was the channel leading to our storage tank.

All around us were the signs of past activity. Above were remains of kilns that had turned limestone into plaster. Once there had been another hamlet above us, but the only indication was a cave more recently used as a stable. When our track was bulldozed, Moorish burials were uncovered. We picked up a broken piece of Moorish water pipe. Trumpet-shaped, the two foot long clay sections slotted into each other. The design was perfectly adapted to extremes of climate, expanding and contracting to stay watertight whatever the weather.

New water pipes were an issue. A campaign to prevent water being piped away from the Alpujarra was lost while we were there. It was argued, and not unreasonably, that if water was not being used, it should be taken to a place where it would be – the coast. From high in the mountains the path of the buried pipeline is marked by a tear in the landscape, the dun colour of the abandoned *cortijos* up there. Where it crosses a river bed, the pipe is encased in concrete. None of this is pleasing to the eye.

Water pipelines raise the emotional intensity that building a road across an Oxford meadow or Twyford Down does in England. A few Alpujarran roadside rocks became bill boards for protest. *'No al trasvase.'* Down on the coast feeling ran equally high. When water which Salobreña thought it deserved was piped to Almuñécar instead, the mayor of Salobreña went on hunger strike. To support her, people blocked the coastal highway. But journalists' attention soon faltered: in Almuñécar there was an outbreak of poisoning and the new water supply was blamed.

Among our earliest guests at Las Monjas were Lynda and Lars Pranger. Lynda was a delicate Englishwoman who studied art and went on to become a writer and a translator of Spanish poetry. Her husband Lars, Swedish and an accomplished painter who had exhibited regularly in Paris, had an impish smile and a humour to match. They lived in a house overlooking the valley of the river Trevélez. It was the summer home of Gerald Brenan, who died in 1987 aged ninety-two, his last home in the Alpujarra although we did not know that when we first visited. Lynda was Brenan's companion and carer during his last two decades, supported by Lars in the latter years.

Although curious about aspects of Brenan's life, and the veracity of parts of *South from Granada*, we held back. At the time we were not planning a book and were cautious about spoiling a tender new friendship. We waited for Brenan to fall naturally into the conversation which, in time, he did. Instead, we talked of writers and writing, of Spain and Spaniards. Lynda was returning to her poetry now that her children, Carlos and Emily, were growing older. She was typically modest, but her translations of St John of the Cross were vigorously praised when they were published in the seventies.

CHAPTER TWENTY-TWO

COUNTRY
WINE

IF BY RARE CHANCE you see a bottle of red wine made from the vigiriega grape, buy it. And drink it cool, not as a curiosity but for its evocation of the dry stony mountain where the fruit ripened among herbs.

Only because a handful of peasant winemakers kept on their vigiriega vines, for a century since phyloxera almost wiped them out, is one able to taste the wine now. A small quantity of these grapes are mixed in the must of many varieties to make their versions of the rosé of the coastal Contraviesa mountain range, *vino de la costa*. *Costa* is seldom to be enjoyed further away than Granada.

It is an acquired taste. Forget the pale rosés of Anjou, this is a tough wine for tough people. Poverty and conservatism have kept them making wine here;

Country Wine

years ago.

On the poor and permeable schistose soil, vines
yield at least a third fewer grapes than in Spain's
favoured wine-growing areas. Machinery cannot be
used: the land is too steep.

During the nineteenth century business boomed
and land under cultivation increased six fold. Wine
and brandy were shipped to far parts of the country
and used to fortify sherry for its journey to England.
Then the plague struck, and poverty. People emigrated to South America and Algeria. The population
of Albondón, one of the main towns of the Contraviesa, dropped from 4,228 in 1877 to 828 in 1900. Land
was sold for the equivalent of fifteen pence an acre.
Farmers planted almond trees in the vineyards. Winemaking continued for local consumption. As the vines
died – eighty per cent were fifty years or more old –
costa might have gone too. There are cheaper wines
available in supermarket cartons. Instead *costa* survived long enough to be saved by those twin conser-
vationists: tourism and the ecology movement.

This is all irrelevant to dedicated *costa* drinkers like
Miguel. Andrew met him on a walk up to the village
for bread, and returned uncertainly, a loaf in one hand
and a Coca-Cola bottle in the other, his straw hat
tipped back.

'I met a man in the street. He was having some
costa delivered and insisted I had a glass.'

'Just one?'

Andrew admitted to several. 'Miguel, he's called.
His cousin over on the Contraviesa makes the wine.

171

It's good. He gave me some to bring home.' He held out the bottle, a third full of pink wine.

Lesley liked it too which was unusual as she frequently found *costa* unpalatable: 'Thick and sour like that red cough mixture we used to have when we were children. Same colour too.'

We usually bought ours from a winemaker in the village of Torvizcón, in a modern demijohn encased in plastic rather than wicker. Full sized jars contained sixteen litres or an *arroba*, from the Arabic *ar-rub* meaning a quarter (of a *quintal*, another Arabic word meaning a hundred and weighing almost the same as an Imperial hundredweight).

The *bodega* doubled as a bar. The day we set out to find it, men were sitting in the entrance drinking beer which made us doubt we had come to the correct place. We saw only a whitewashed passage and a doorway to a barely furnished office. As there was no one more promising, we explained to the group: 'We'd like to buy some wine.'

One man detached himself from the group. 'Come this way.' He led us along the passage into a large, dark room where huge barrels stood. 'Old or new wine?'

'May we try some?'

'Of course.' Dusty glasses were located in the gloom and given a quick wipe with a handy cloth. Rose coloured liquid was drawn from a barrel. Lesley sipped. Andrew took a good mouthful. He emptied the small straight sided tumbler and handed it back. The man went to the other barrel.

'And the Señora?' But Lesley clung to her glass while giving Andrew her 'and you be careful' look.

He swallowed a mouthful of the second wine. Then: 'I prefer the first. Is it the new or the old?'

'New, from the last harvest.'

We bought a quarter *arroba*, and blinked our way into the sunshine from the coolness of the *bodega*. That *costa* was good but with 300 producers wine is bound to be variable. You can be served good *costa* in an old whisky bottle in a bar and bad wine in a pretty earthenware jug in a smart restaurant.

We had met an elderly man, a neighbour of friends, in a village high on the Contraviesa. He insisted we taste the wine he made for his family and friends. We praised its depth of flavour.

'Tate Montoya couldn't have done better than us,' whispered Lesley.

Montoya, one of Andalusia's most popular enter-tainers, presented *Tal Como Somos*, 'Just As We Are', which we renamed 'Down Your Pueblo', remembering the BBC radio programme, 'Down Your Way', which had a similar concept. Montoya put everyone at ease, tapped his feet to the local bands and never upstaged his subjects. He let them get the laughs.

One day he was interviewing an old man who pro-duced a bottle of home made *costa*. Montoya passed the supreme test. Sipping, he controlled his face and managed a smiling '*unico*', unique.

Wine made from the vigiriega grapes alone is in a different class from *costa*. We drove up to Barranco Oscuro, the dark gully, where this rare grape grows. Inside the modern winery of the Contralp Co-operative were lofty stainless steel tanks, a contrast to the rustic *bodega* at Torvizcón. The man we had come to meet was Francisco Molina, winemaker. He was younger than we expected, his office spacious enough for meetings of the twenty-three members of the co-operative.

Contralp was one of the fruits of the Department of Agriculture and the economic development plan for the Alpujarra. The department has recognized that making high quality products for which people would be willing to pay well was the surest way to protect jobs in the region. The co-operative was founded in 1987 to implement the plan to restructure the region's vineyards; transform land to organic production; restore the vigiriega grape; and to improve the social economy.

Molina held up two bottles from the display of the half dozen varieties they made. 'These two wines are similar. This one is organic and we sell it for half as much again as the other. Organic production is more profitable.

'At the moment half our output is organic wines, but we are increasing the proportion. These are the wines we sell in France and Germany, Madrid and Barcelona where that quality is important.'

He explained that, traditionally, little fertilizer had been used in the vineyards and so it had been relatively easy to move away from artificial ones. Also the high altitude of the vineyards protected them from attack by most insects. Organic wines were exploiting a natural advantage.

From the winery we went on to visit Manuel Valenzuela, the man on whose initiative the co-operative was founded. He lived nearby, down a gentle slope past the plot of newly planted vigiriega vines. The variety is unique to the area and makes the full-bodied red, flinty wine we had tasted a few minutes earlier.

There was no one at the house. We wondered whether he was the bearded man we saw driving the other way when we stopped at a fork deciding which road to take. He came back. Valenzuela had been on his way to meet someone and did not have much time to spare. Lesley felt the interview might be easier if she kept out of the way so she waited in the car. But he seemed to forget about being in a hurry and loved to talk about winemaking. He was no longer a member of the co-operative. Andalusians, he said, were not as good at co-operating as the people of northern Spain, but he betrayed no rancour. 'The people here are more individual.'

He took Andrew into an untidy office, where he hoped to show some magazine cuttings. In the jumble he could not find the right file. He said he had known about winemaking all his life because his father made wine. 'It was not good wine,' he added with a smile. Then they went through the long farmhouse kitchen and down into the cellar. This was reminiscent of the *bodega* at Torvizcón, with wooden barrels in a dark room. But Valenzuela made smooth chardonnays and pinot noirs.

After they had talked, Andrew bought some bottles, and Valenzuela made him a gift of another, an unlabelled wine. He said: 'We make this to drink ourselves. It's not bad.' And then he was gone, late for his appointment.

'Who else was in there?' asked Lesley. She had heard two men conversing easily in Spanish and wondered when Andrew was going to edge his way in.

'Just Manuel and myself.'

'But I heard two Spanish voices.'

'You have a bad ear for the Spanish language,' said Andrew, but privately he was pleased.

That evening we opened the wine Valenzuela made for himself. It was *costa*, the wine of the country.

CHAPTER TWENTY-THREE

EVERYTHING UNDER THE SUN

IT MADE SENSE. Yes, it made absolute sense to move the saint's day. What, after all, is the point of having a party when no one can come? 'The Queen of England has real and official birthdays, so why shouldn't our village?' Isabella at the shop was explaining why the patronal festival of St Mark was celebrated in the middle of August, while the prayer book says it falls on April 25.

'There are few people here then. In August everyone comes home,' she said.

They return from Barcelona, Madrid, foreign lands and the cities and coast of Andalusia. They come back in their thousands for the holiday month. At the end of it there is the complementary phenomenon, the weekend of the exodus of the *retornados*.

In the evenings the handful of Carataunas people who normally took a walk – a *paseo* – were augmented by dozens more. Young couples took toddlers and babies in push-chairs. Everyone put on their smart clothes and went for a stroll. There was a nice level walk from the village to the *mirador*, the view point, where the village sign was set into a curved wall built in the form of a seat. Actually, resting there meant turning away from the view and watching traffic on the main road, but no one except us appeared to think that was crazy. Anyway the purpose of the outing was to chat. People kept it up for hours, well into the night. Teenagers climbed a *camino* to another wall near a restaurant on the road. The girls sat, like a line of cut out paper dolls, picked out by the headlights of passing cars. Some distance away stood the boys.

The day of the fiesta arrived. Grandmothers were in their element. 'Encarnación . . . No, the other Encarnación, the cousin of Rosa . . . That's right, Pilar's daughter. She's got married and has a lovely baby, Diana . . .' The group had pulled two tables together on the grassy space that was the nearest thing we saw to an English village green. One of the men looked bored and whispered to another. 'More drinks,' he said and sloped off to the bar.

We did not need to hear every word. We knew the conversation from wedding parties in the Rhondda where Lesley's family lives. Whenever, wherever, emigrants return, it is the same.

A young couple had heard it all before. They got up and walked out of the pool of light. They were too young to remember that in 1959 Spanish bishops felt able to say: 'Couples walking along arm-in-arm cannot be accepted.' A few years later a more liberal priest warned women: 'Whenever you kiss a man, remember your last communion and think to yourself: "Could the Sacred Host and the lips of this man come together without sacrilege?" ' In those years when the majority of young people counted themselves practising Catholics, only one in ten believed premarital sex acceptable. Since the death of Franco they have become as free as any in Europe.

Our summons to the fiesta had been a salvo of rockets fired over the house. We reached the top of the hill in time to see St Mark making his swaying progress out of the square and alongside the green. Turning left by the bar, he passed the old school and the new health centre, and went on to the threshing circle, the village *era*, for a wonderful open view after his months among golden baroque. It looked like a pagan ceremony, in the midst of that stone circle, a henge without uprights. And all the time rockets were exploding overhead to scare away evil spirits.

Bigger villages had fancier festivals. At Bubión, another village that had made its saint's day a movable fiesta, we tagged on to a procession through the lower part of the village. Ahead of us, lit by dim street lights, was a figure borne on the shoulders of young men. A newly formed children's band played and their friends sang. When the procession paused, a round-faced and corpulent man preached at us from a doorstep. He used the sing-song of the litany to recite the sins of *El Zorro*: the wrongdoings of the fox and the number of chickens he had taken.

Everyone laughed. The 'priest' splashed the crowd with 'holy water' and a young man near us lifted a skin wine bottle and expertly directed a stream of liquid into his mouth. He handed the bottle to Andrew who lifted it and squeezed. His aim was perfect, *costa* sprayed on the back of his throat. Through his fit of coughing, he choked his *gracias* and returned the bottle to its owner.

The image at the head of the procession was a stuffed fox. The occasion was fun for the young people and ended with the mock priest burying the animal. What did it symbolize? Brenan, who recorded a similar event in Yegen, believed it signified burying the old year. Perhaps that was true, as the original date of the Bubión fiesta had been in January.

August is the best month for fiestas. Night is the time to live, when the fierce heat of day has faded. You can dance until dawn if you wish and many do. Unfortunately, those who need sleep suffer because the way travelling bands attracted bookings was by advertising the high decibel levels.

At Las Monjas bands and discos rarely bothered us although occasionally we were woken by music from miles away. We were comfortable too, the breeze of an electric fan cooling us as we slept. In our bedroom night temperatures stayed in the nineties and we slept with, at most, a sheet over us.

'ANDREW, *WHAT* HAVE YOU done to the water?' When anything goes wrong Lesley's instinct leads her to what she believes is the source of the problem. Taps were tested. There was a mere gurgle. 'The spring must have run dry,' said Andrew who was so afraid of this happening, he had put off checking the flow. No point, he thought, in anticipating a crisis. But what were we to do now? We could not ferry sufficient water in our plastic containers for all our needs. Life would be unbearable without baths and in August every habitable building was occupied. We would not find anywhere else to live.

The crisis was short-lived but it gave way to mystery. Our tank was empty although water continued to flow into it. None of the holiday homes in the abandoned hamlet was occupied. The pipes did not leak. One clue: plants had been cut back near one of the houses. That had to be it. Someone had been in there and used a lot of water.

As no one was around, we left a grumbling letter pinned on the door. Gradually the tank refilled and thirty-six hours later there was enough pressure to work our taps again. It was a long thirty-six hours but we were too hot to worry. We collected extra water from the spring on the main road and bathed by plunging into our pool. By then we were experts at keeping the house cool, closing shutters in rotation as the sun moved round the house, and opening them to catch the cooling breeze that came down from the mountains after the direction of the air flow changed at sundown.

Up at dawn after the hottest nights, we discovered that the night air had hardly made a difference and the stone slabs of the terrace retained the previous day's warmth. We settled into a routine of rising early and working either until we went into a town at mid-morning, or until we were ready for lunch at around 3 p.m. After that we read and perhaps slept until the worst of the heat had passed. Sometimes we watched television. Summer schedules meant that prime time programmes were broadcast then. Only cotton or linen clothes were wearable and bearable.

We discussed travelling north, to cool green Galicia perhaps. 'But the car doesn't have air conditioning. It would be hell getting there.'

'All right, we'll drive through the nights.'

'That's hardly a good way to see Spain!'

Before we had decided, the temperature dropped down to the nineties and we had a few days of relative coolness before it soared again and we reopened discussions. In the end we didn't go anywhere, we learned to live with it.

Bertie, our friends' cat, was with us for five weeks that summer. He liked to sprawl on stone floors, legs stuck out. To us, used to seeing northern cats coiled into cosy balls, he looked extraordinary. He did not know how to eat anything that did not come out of a packet or a tin, and expected to be cuddled like a human baby with his head in the crooks of our arms.

A green orange dangling like a pompon over the edge of the terrace became his plaything. He kicked fallen olives around too. When he lost one he clambered up a favourite tree, chose a fresh toy and carried it down in his mouth.

We kept a thermometer in the shade of a pillar on the terrace. Some afternoons it rose to 110°F. Limbs and brain just stopped. Everything stopped. The thing we noticed most about the heat was the silence. Only crickets buzzing in the olive trees kept going. Goat bells fell silent. The whoops of children playing in a swimming pool down in Bayacas dwindled away.

Dogs and birds snoozed in shade. Roads were empty. It was quieter than night.

When the weather is like that, you retreat indoors. You switch off electric lights because the heat they generate is discernible. For the first time we appreciated houses with windowless rooms.

In winter you can pile more logs on the fire on the coldest days, add extra clothing, warm yourself with hot drinks. There is far less you can do about heat, without succumbing to extravagant and ecologically questionable air conditioning. In summer you have only a fan to swish the hot air around, a leisurely lunch and then a siesta. The siesta is not laziness but self-preservation.

Evenings are for talking, perhaps taking a walk and eating. But you do not feel like eating until it is cooler, ten o'clock or later. After that, you are ready to enjoy the night. In August there were many attractions in addition to fiestas. Folk music in the bars, for instance, because home-comers are nostalgic. In our nearest bar-restaurant parties of ten or twelve dipped into communal plates of ham and *chorizo* set down on the tables between their car radios. They had brought from Barcelona their city crime prevention habits.

Yet again we were glad we had moved house, because down in the valley they were suffering from humidity as the sun dried the heavily irrigated land. Valley people were the first to escape to the hills at weekends. One Sunday we spotted Mari Carmen from the market, standing beneath chestnut trees on the road up the mountains.

'It was fresher there,' she said when we next spoke to her. 'It's too hot here.'

Half the world seemed to be in the mountains that Sunday so we had changed our plans and not gone very high. We dared not risk sitting in a traffic jam beneath blazing sun on Europe's highest road. Instead we took that road to Granada one weekday by mistake. After lunch at the Las Terrazas in Bubión we had started the journey home when Lesley said: 'Why go down into the heat when we can go up into fresh air? We could take the top road to Trevélez, if we can find it.'

'I'm sure we can.'

So we turned round and drove up through Capileira, wincing at the ugly tourist development along the road.

Above the village we breathed the resinous scent of the pine forests and came to a sign warning that the road was suitable only for four-wheel drive vehicles and small cars. We were safe on both counts. The drivers of an American convertible and two Mercedes which sailed past us believed they were too. Soon we had left the trees behind and were among boulders. The land was damp and cattle grazed green patches. The road was unsurfaced and we had to close our windows against the clouds of dust following cars coming in the opposite direction. At a view point we stopped. Far down below lay Trevélez, the highest village in Spain and famous for the hams cured in its cool air.

'Oh!'

'Yes, I know. We've missed the turn. We're on our way to Granada.'

'But have we got enough petrol for that?'

'We ought to make it, just.'

We caught up with the American convertible, in trouble on the loose surface of a not very steep incline. One of the Mercedes was already turning back. We felt smug in our cheap Suzuki as we left them behind. This southern side of the mountain was not especially steep because the scarp, leading down to Granada, was on the other side of the pass. The road was cut into the side of a great stony bowl. In a short while the grey treeless landscape was broken up by mountain lakes. A heat haze prevented us seeing as far as the coast, let alone Africa.

We walked around one of the lakes. The breeze was definitely, delightfully cool. At first glance the broken rocky earth looked barren but then we noticed beautiful blue alpine flowers growing in the cracks. The water was icy. Floating in the middle was equipment for measuring pollution. As the air smelled so pure, it seemed improbable there could be anything to measure, and yet we had seen the pollution problem for ourselves. One day on the Lújar we happened to look across to the Sierra Nevada at exactly the moment when a plume of dirty yellow petro-chemical smog rose above the mountains from Granada.

On through the rocky landscape. At one point we headed for a cliff wall, a barrier of stone with no way round. Above and to the right was the Veleta, 11,145 feet high, the second highest peak of the massif. Closing in on the cliff, we at last saw a way through. A pass had been cut below the Veleta, a few hundred feet above us. Soon we were through, gazing across mountains and mountains beyond mountains. This had long been our image of Spain, a land of vast landscapes and endless mountains. Below lay Granada and the fertile green apron of its Vega.

Driving down the scarp was harder work. We spun through hairpins. This is where they ski in winter. Out of season it would pass for a quarry, complete with aerial ropeways like those once used to carry colliery waste and dump it on the mountains. A bulldozer was gouging a new run. Pictures of winter sports, all that freshness and cleanliness and healthiness, had not prepared us for this destruction. Eventually we left behind Sol y Nieve and drove down into the heat, slowly, eking out the petrol. We rolled up to a filling station between the ski slopes and the city.

On our way home we stopped at a Granada hypermarket. Air-conditioned shopping. That is the other thing you can do on an August day in Andalusia.

CHAPTER TWENTY-FOUR

THE MILLER
AND THE POTTER

A PACK OF DOGS growled as we reached the mill but the man who emerged was happy to see us. 'Of course you may look around.'

The room was square, walls white with *cal*, floor white with flour. The stone revolved. A stream of maize fell from a chute and was guided by a carved wooden hand into a hole in the top stone. Flour poured from between the grindstones.

Maria, the miller, took us to see the tower down which water poured to power it. It was, she confirmed, the last working grain mill near Órgiva. The turbine mechanism was believed to have been introduced by the Romans. The mill is on the river Sucio at Las Barreras. By coincidence the most ancient pottery in the area is there too.

Antonio Orellana Romera, better known as Cache-riche, was equally welcoming. He was famous as the latest of the line of potters, stretching back into antiquity, to make the practical pots of everyday life. The Moorish kiln was still in use. His wheel was 300 years old.

The workshop had a dry, spicy smell totally unlike the musty clay you sniff in a British pottery. Cache-riche, a solid man whose chubby fingers seemed too clumsy to form the smaller objects, handed us examples of earthenware. Rough surfaces, not yet smoothed by oil and handling, were warm like the stones outside. Their lines, determined by centuries of practical demands, were pleasing, often elegant. He loosened a pot sherd from an earth bank. 'Moorish,' he said. The Romans were in the valley too, no doubt you can also pick up their rejects.

One of the things he passed to us defeated our imaginations. If we had seen it in a museum labelled 'Votive Object' we would not have blinked. But he had a row of them. Each had a small body above a large skirt. The skirt, a cone of baked clay, had two segments cut out on opposite sides. At the top sat a round container with an opening and a lip.

'A *tonto*,' he said.

That was no clue, just confusion because it means silly. '*Loco?*' we asked, using the word meaning crazy.

He nodded.

'But what is it for?'

He slipped his fingers through the divided skirt. 'It's a lamp for lighting bread ovens and looking in dark corners.' He bent and demonstrated peering at the back of a shelf.

Cacheriche continues to make *tontos*, nearly two centuries after the invention of the match. Things can take a long time to catch on in the Alpujarra. His *candiles*, oil lamps, might have been those for which the biblical wise virgin reserved her oil. And his objects of ancient design had been in daily use until a very few years ago. That was why his father taught him the family trade. We saw his water bottles, unglazed to allow evaporation, used by men in the fields, although all the people who knocked at our door for refills carried plastic bottles.

'This is unique,' said Cacheriche, holding up a flat sided bottle with two loops, 'the *cantina Rio Chico*.' He demonstrated how a shepherd could hang it on a cord across his shoulder. One day we saw a man using one of these. Usually, though, his customers were tourists. He tipped his head in the direction of the Poqueira villages where the coaches call. 'They sell them up there for twice what I charge. I get dealers from Barcelona buying from me too.' He smiled a knowing smile. None of us dared suggest that they reappeared across Spain as antiques.

A well-dressed man interrupted. He bought the most handsome water bottle, tall with clean lines, one Lesley had her eye on. Then he wanted to take a photograph. Cacheriche had done it before, many times: he posed beside the wheel with the ease of a supermodel. This other customer came from a distant part of Spain, Valdepeñas, and was a collector. He bought pots whenever he travelled and his wife had ruled there could be no more in the house, so he was setting up a museum.

Recognizing in Andrew an aficionado, he opened

the back of his car and showed us everything he had bought on his current trip: bottles and jugs of all shapes and sizes in different coloured clays; some rough, some fine. He was particularly proud of a jug with its neck extended in a goffered collar. The workmanship was good but we did not think the prissy design suited practical earthenware. Our friend from Valdepeñas extolled its virtues at length. Cacheriche was too polite to state his opinion, chipping in a non-committal '*claro*', of course, when invited to back up the man's enthusiasm. But he was not expected to say much, the other experts were too busy talking.

When we got back home with our selection of *tontos* and *candiles* and a *cantina Rio Chico*, the goats were crossing the track by the house. The goatherd was young, good-looking and remote. Most goatherds welcomed the chance to break their solitude and talk but not this one. We cannot remember ever managing a conversation with him, although he replied to a greeting and returned a wave. He was different from most in another way: he carried his belongings in a leather rucksack, the kind that was trendy and expensive in cities, and he used field glasses.

Before we had moved in, he had enjoyed free run of our land. Goats had chewed young orange trees down to stumps and knocked stones from terrace walls. Once we were living there, he automatically kept them off, taking them behind the house. On the terrace behind was a fig tree with a branch overhanging our roof. Soon the goats discovered it was a bridge to reach self-seeded plants growing out of our *launa*.

One evening we were shooing them off when a Norwegian man called to explain why our tank had run dry. We had pinned our plea on his door. Apparently the man from Bayacas, whom he employed to look after his house, had discovered the normal water supply was broken. Using his initiative he had taken water from the only other source – our deposit. This had left nobody happy. The Norwegian was not pleased because, as he said: 'It's bad water. I had it analysed and wouldn't use it. You shouldn't either.'

We were not unduly surprised. Our clothes came scratchy with lime from the wash, dark clothes were streaked with grey. We assured him we did not drink it nor cook with it, but he insisted we should not wash with it either. We had no choice, there was no one else's supply for us to filch.

Down in Bayacas, a hundred feet below on the valley bottom, a farmer ploughed with oxen. The dun beasts plodded, as a man guided the iron tipped wooden plough. The carpenter might have taken his pattern from an ancient Egyptian stone carving or a Greek vase. Once again, we had that sense of moving back in time. When the ploughman called to the oxen he used unfamiliar words, not Spanish dictionary words. No, like much of the agricultural language of the Alpujarra, the words that commanded the beasts in the fields were of Arabic origin.

As the field turned from yellow dust to brown, a second man broadcast seeds from an esparto basket held tilted at his hip. He raised a handful of seeds, and cast them with a sweep of his arm, again and again. Andrew got as far as fetching his camera but then had doubts and did not walk down to the field. Intrude and you break the spell.

'Another day,' he said.

But there are no two country days the same. The tasks, the shadows, the demeanour of the actors in the drama, all would be different another day. He meant he was not going to do it at all.

We watched as the ploughing and sowing were completed and the plough was unhitched from the yoke. Then a log of wood, a foot in diameter, six feet long and flattened on one side, was tied behind the animals. A man rode it, balanced like a water skier, as the oxen dragged it around the field. Ridges were flattened, seeds buried. Finally, the plough was used to create a couple of graceful curved channels to carry irrigation water to all parts of the field.

Over the next weeks that field turned green and then gold. Men came with sickles and cut the barley, standing the straw-tied sheaves in stooks. To us, used to the pace of a northern climate, all this happened with remarkable speed.

In the last century Richard Ford complained that Andalusian farmers were slow to use improved farm equipment. Brenan recorded that 'The economy of an Alpujarran village had scarcely changed since medieval times. And the instruments of husbandry were of an even greater antiquity.'

Seventy years on, the traditions linger although Rotovators have become more common than ploughs drawn by mule or oxen. Unfortunately, a Rotovator does not merely mean work is done faster. Until one starts up, the sounds of the countryside at work are what they always were: the subdued clacking of hand tools; the rhythmic hooves of a mule with its burden; a man's repetitive talk to his animals; the rush of water along an *acequia*; and someone, somewhere sending his voice floating far out across the land. When a machine starts up, there is nothing but a machine to listen to.

ANDREW WENT TO THE Obelix bar one day to collect a photographic print we had bought in an exhibition there. He was in the back bar when he heard familiar voices. James and Elena. They were trying to borrow money on the security of a Dutch note. Joining them he caught up with their news. They had survived only a week as buskers in Granada. They had been to the Netherlands, working on the land to earn money for a trip to India. In India they had bought silver bangles to sell in Spain.

'Have you seen José?' asked James.

'We hope he might have work for James,' Elena added.

It was a shock to be asked. 'Haven't you heard? He's dead.'

'He was,' said James, 'a good man. A kind man.' Then he asked if he could borrow a small sum.

A thin end of a wedge, Andrew feared. But he handed over the money and waved away the Dutch note proffered in exchange. 'Early next week we will pay you back, once we have sold some bracelets,' said Elena. 'Thank you.' She bowed her forehead to her fingertips.

When Andrew told the story to Lesley he missed out the bit about the money. He did not expect to see it back and it was a slight salve to his conscience for leaving them out in the storm.

CHAPTER TWENTY-FIVE

EYE OF THE BEHOLDER

ONE OF THE DELIGHTS of Las Monjas was walking out into the countryside, through herbs and terraces of olives and almonds. In one direction we plunged down a path into the virtually deserted valley of the river Seco. The name means dry but it is one of the best watered valleys, rich and green under the shade of ancient olives. The main Órgiva *acequia* runs through it, a fast flowing channel on the valley side until it tunnels through rocks into the next valley. There is even a flyover in the middle of a green wood where one *acequia* goes over another. The houses here are abandoned for no road has ever been cut into the valley of the Seco.

In front of our house the track winds down to the broad Chico valley. Turn left at the bottom and a well defined path leads to Órgiva, hidden from us by a hill. Turn right and there is a steep-sided sylvan valley. Dykes were built early this century to tame the flash floods this apparently feeble mountain stream could bring.

At the top of one of these dykes is a spring. It pulses water to the surface with the roar of an underground force: one moment gently bubbling and the next stirring the pool like a freezing Jacuzzi. Close by was once a village called Barjas, swept away by flood water in 1856. We could find nothing of it except a mule path leading up the mountain from the spring. This is a remarkable *camino de herradura*, or horseshoe path, which remained in good condition, saved because it goes nowhere important. It moves through the forest in perfectly engineered zig-zags, the gradients never too steep. At one point a stone causeway eases it over a shallow valley. The surface of flat stones remained in sound condition, a memorial to the skill of those who built it.

Above the trees, where there is agricultural land, the path is decayed and difficult to follow. We lost our way when walking to Soportújar, nearly 600 feet above Carataunas, and needed guidance. An old man sat under a tree with his sack by his side. Lesley thought he was a tramp.

'I'm going to Soportújar now. I'll show you.' He slung the sack over his shoulder and leaped up the slope at a terrific pace. He took short cuts, scrambling up the edges of terraces with the agility of a goat. We panted behind him. Questions, questions, that was the way to slow him.

'Is there no *camino* to the village?'

'Yes but this way is shorter.' He sprang up to the next terrace.

'You come out here every day?' Andrew hardly had breath for words and Lesley was trailing.

'Yes, I have land.'

'There are few people to work the land now.' Around us there were few signs of recent cultivation.

He took the comment as a criticism. 'We work in the fields every day.' He found fresh energy and quickened the pace.

Ahead was a dark green square, with plants growing on wires. 'Raspberries? You grow raspberries here?'

'Oh yes. They're more profitable.'

Raspberries are not a fruit one associates with southern Spain; the first canes were planted ten years ago. The experimental agricultural station at Lanjarón, while selecting crops to provide employment and reduce emigration, discovered that raspberries grow well on high land. A quarter of the Spanish crop, tiny compared with those of Germany and Britain, now comes from the Alpujarra. Most goes into jam. We puffed past the raspberry patch.

A black and white mongrel dog saved us. He ran up, tail wagging. It looked like a daily ritual as the man sat down, untied his sack, took out half a loaf of bread and fed it to the dog. We went through the usual minuet about whether we had children and whether we paid much rent. Then Andrew, looking far down the valley, said: 'It's very beautiful.' He used the words *muy precioso*, a phrase reserved for the highest praise.

'Yes, the land down there is very rich.' He patted the dog.

'But now there's the first greenhouse.' Andrew pointed to a white pond of plastic shimmering in the sunlight. We could see it from our house too, the shadow of a change we hated. Raspberries we liked, sensible agricultural development that suited the landscape and people, but plasticulture was unsightly revolution.

'It's most beautiful.' The old man chose the word *bellisimo*. 'It's very profitable.'

He was right about the profits, and 'progressive' farmers had already wrapped parts of the Alpujarra in plastic. We had seen the worst of it. The view across the coastal plain that stretches towards Almeria is startling: an ocean of whiteness that looks like enormous saltings, crystals left by the evaporation of sea water. It is all plastic sheeting.

In the 1840s Richard Ford described crossing 'the dreary sandy plains which might easily be irrigated'. A century and a half later they have been. Where once there were a few hovels there is El Ejido, a town since 1982, with a population of more than 40,000 and growing.

We could not nerve ourselves to stop there, it was too depressing. The main road runs straight for miles flanked by flats, shops, warehouses, manufacturers of plastic and pallets and thousands of acres of plastic greenhouses. It is a hideous place, dedicated to forcing out-of-season peppers and cucumbers for the supermarkets of northern Europe. A billion pounds weight of vegetables are produced in a year and 56 million bunches of flowers, mostly carnations, many sold through the Dutch markets.

El Ejido is the black country of the agricultural revolution. Poisonous smoke curls up from bonfires of old plastic, mingling with air tainted by the indiscriminate use of pesticides. Birds died, possibly from the lack of insects or directly from the chemicals. Men committed suicide after working in humid, chemical laden greenhouses. Young people became addicted to drugs and stole to pay for them. Immigrant labour was exploited. There was a treadmill of pesticide bills and re-investment. El Ejido looked like a plastic bubble that must some day burst.

So we disliked plasticulture and its effect, but we could understand the old man at Soportújar. He had scratched a poor living and had reason to marvel at the plastic innovation that brought farmers shiny new cars, houses with two bathrooms and swimming pools. We parted from him in the village and hurried home before dark by a more direct route. Supper was a simple meal of pasta cooked on a little camping stove because we had forgotten to check the gas bottles.

Next morning Andrew set out early to replace them in Lanjarón and saw Elena hitchhiking. She was going to Lanjarón for a licence to sell bangles in the market there. 'I'm sorry, Andrew, we don't yet have the money to repay you.'

Andrew, who had not really expected them to, had thought it might never be mentioned. But it had been and, although he might have replied that the money was a present, he did not. Instead he asked: 'Could you give me some Spanish lessons?' Since Carmen had given up her weekend teaching, he had been looking for a new tutor. This provided an honourable solution. The loan was less than the price of one lesson, and the arrangement would give Elena and James some income.

CHAPTER TWENTY-SIX

HAM, HAM, HAM

ANDREW'S FIRST LESSON was to be at El Morreon, a travellers' enclave where Elena and James were camped. The track from the town passed the brick-built Moorish olive mill. Although dilapidated, it remained one of the more impressive local buildings. It was for sale: a notice board gave a Barcelona telephone number. Various people were rumoured to have considered it but had been deterred by the price.

The track carried on through olive groves before dropping down into the dry valley of the Sucio, a place of wild flowers, bright with the pink of oleander. El Morreon itself is a tump near the confluence of the Sucio and Guadalfeo. A collection of old buses and vans was parked on a flat area, a place untidy with tatty furniture and the black evidence of fires. Washing flew from lines between vehicles, the homes of travellers from all parts of Europe. Andrew thought that if plans to dam the river went ahead the old houses on the tump would make restaurants with spectacular views of the reservoir.

He got slightly lost and then found Elena, sitting in a garden. She and James had a new tent and were planning to buy a car. She proved to be a tough teacher with an exact knowledge of the grammar of Spanish and English. That she preferred to talk about the beauty of nature and the miracle of life, extended Andrew's vocabulary. They watched vultures – *buitres*, Andrew learned – circling the crag where he had found the castle. No, it was not from the Civil War but Moorish, she told him.

Although Elena and James were staying in El Morreon, they did not fit there and preferred being alone, as they had been on the abandoned land. They did not belong to any group.

Sometimes James announced plans. 'We have to get the car. Then we can do other things, make something of ourselves.' At times he was fatalistic: 'Go with the flow. You have to go with the flow. Know what I mean?'

Elena found serenity in Indian philosophy and was one of the few people we have met who literally would not hurt a fly. Yet lurking below the surface was the influence of her middle-class upbringing in a Buenos Aires suburb, her education and her doctorate in geology at a German university.

Between El Morreon and Bubión there was a gulf in attitudes and interests. One of the pleasures of living in the Alpujarra was that we brushed up against people in all spheres. Bubión was where we moved in the world of art and craft.

'Ham, ham and more ham, that's what the tourists want. They're not interested in art,' said Cristina. We were the only people in the gallery. In Spain ham is more than a food, it is an idea. In a popular film that year, *Jamón, Jamón*, it was a murder weapon.

Cristina looked around. There were few orange sold stickers on the paintings by a leading young artist. The room was a modern construction in the old style with chestnut beams and a prominent fireplace. She and her husband, José María, who ran the Espacio D'Arte together had created a real gallery where good artists were pleased to exhibit. Bubión, Barcelona and Paris do not look out of place together on the c.v. of a rising artist.

A private view in the Alpujarra was not so different from an event in the capital cities of art. A waiter moved around the groups with a tray of wine, although it was *costa* instead of chablis. Voices were from all parts of Spain and Europe, because most were *forasteros*, incomers. Many were themselves painters or craftsmen and craftswomen like Cristina, who sells dried flower arrangements, and her husband, a potter.

A small proportion of tourists were knowledgeable and bought paintings or the excellent pottery, fabrics and basketwork produced locally. But most chose the popular, and now debased, Granada pottery. Cristina was right when she said they came for ham. In a survey more than four out of five named it when asked about holiday preferences. That was double the number who mentioned *costa*. Handmade fabrics were well down, behind sausages. Pottery was beaten by honey.

It was nothing new for tourists to go to the Alpujarra for ham. Richard Ford wrote in his 1845 guide:

'Up in the mountains is Trevélez where the *jamones dulces de las Alpujarras* are cured: no gastronome should neglect these sweet hams. Very little salt is used; the ham is placed eight days in a weak pickle, and then hung up in the snow; while at Berja and in the less elevated places, more salt is used, and the delicate flavour destroyed.

'The hamlet of Trevélez (population about 1,500) is situated among these mountains, and is only one league south east from the top of the Mulhacén. The whole of the taa (district) is wild and Alpine; the trout in the river Trevélez are delicious.'

In a later edition, he complained about the filthy accommodation in Trevélez. Poverty stricken, most of the people could not afford meat. The ham they produced from acorn fed pigs was sublime, and for sale.

When we first saw Trevélez, in its narrow wooded valley, it looked much like other villages in the Alpujarra. White buildings cascaded to the river, the uppermost houses several hundred feet above the lowest. Unsurprisingly there is dispute over the altitude of the village but at around 4,900 feet it is the highest in Spain. As we approached we realized it was out of scale. Modern curing factories had broken the harmony of the flat-roofed houses.

We first went there one New Year's Day with a

vegetarian friend. Vegetable stews, once the staple, had been forgotten. All dishes, except a potato omelette, incorporated ham. We ate on a terrace, something for our friend to boast about back in London: 'On New Year's Day we sat outside in the sun in Spain's highest village for lunch. Over the other side of the mountain they were skiing.' In the shade, Andrew snapped off a six inch icicle.

Crisp air and snow are what made Trevélez hams famous. In the nineteenth century Queen Isabel II, who was to be deposed in one of Spain's attempts at democracy, gave the area the right to use a special stamp of quality on its hams, a sort of 'By Royal Appointment'. Empress Eugénie, wife of Napoleon III, is said to have introduced Trevélez ham to the French court. Rossini, a cook (some say a glutton) as well as the composer of *The Barber of Seville*, preferred Trevélez ham to that of York or Westphalia.

Unfortunately, none of them would recognize much of the ham produced today in Trevélez and the neighbouring villages, allowed to use the name. Big business, it beats tourism into second place and between them they account for two thirds of the economy. With that has come change and a decline in flavour. Ham has long been a much loved luxury product in Spain. One of the writers who praised it was Baltasar del Alcazar who in the sixteenth century wrote these revealing lines:

204

There are three things
that hold my heart love's captive:
the fair Ines, mountain ham,
and aubergines with cheese.

Ham, Ham, Ham

In the Alpujarra more than 400,000 hams have been cured each year and the output is being increased to around 600,000. Fresh meat is shipped in, not because the process is different elsewhere now that modern meat factories are being used, but so that the name Trevélez can be applied. The Spanish pig with black markings and hooves does not grow fast enough for industrial producers and so the Belgian Landrace had taken over in Spain as it has in Britain. But whatever the breed the custom of fattening the family pig for Christmas continues. One of our most startling memories is of driving round a bend near Órgiva to see a beast strung up and being sliced to pieces outside a *cortijo*.

We usually bought our ham in one of the supermarkets in town, a family business that cured its own. Cutting ham was men's work. If mother was alone behind the counter, there was no ham. Daughter would reluctantly cut a few slices. Son went to work with gusto. Father was the artist.

He would check the row of cut hams, pared close to the bone with meat dry and ideal for flavouring stews. No good. He would disappear and come back with a whole ham. He plunged in a long skewer as though it was a sword – Don Quixote never aspired to greater style. Then he raised the skewer to his nose and inhaled deeply, eyes misting with pleasure. Only then could the cutting begin. First the fat was cut away and then a small piece of red meat taken. It went into his mouth to be chewed slowly and as the flavour was released he would smile.

Another piece was cut and handed across the counter. Andrew would take it and, after ritual chewing,

205

pronounce it good. It always was. After weighing, some of the fat would be added to the package as a gift.

On other days an already cut ham was judged to be right. The pieces came off, the knife following the grain of the meat. The scale showed 220 grams.

'You said 150 grams?'

'Yes.'

Slices were lifted off until the requested weight and price registered. Then they were put on again. 'Just the trimmings.' Another gift.

HIGH ROAD
TO YEGEN

THE FIRST CLOUDS came in low. They drifted up the valley like a flight of airships, some above us and a few below. Then as the Chico valley narrowed, there was nowhere for them to go. They hung around outside our front door, like kids on a street corner. Higher clouds collided with the mountains for hours and filled the sky with slate grey. Mountain peaks and then Cáñar, less than a thousand feet above us, were obscured. Raindrops rattled through the leaves of the oranges and evaporated on the hot earth. The scent that rose from the land was heady, invigorating.

But it had happened before. Clouds drifted, leaked a little and floated away, taking their precious rain with them. Sometimes we had seen lightning flashes as storms broke higher up.

207

One day towards the end of summer the clouds stayed and all at once the trickle became a rush. Water poured off the roof. Standing on the terrace was like being behind a mountain waterfall. Inevitably the water found our weak spots and crept down inside walls. It was Andrew's turn to stamp about on the roof. That done, we settled down to read, safe and dry.

But a worry nibbled at our minds. Lesley voiced it first: 'Will our track be washed away?'

'Of course not. There's been worse rain than this.'

There was a point on the track where previous rains and the tramp of goats had cut a downward path. One more foot of erosion and the track would be difficult, two and the jeep would be trapped. After a while Andrew admitted he was thinking about it too. 'I'll go and take a look.'

There was more water on the track than we had seen in most rivers. A torrent rushed down the wheel ruts and then scoured escape routes to the side. In theory dirt roads have diagonal bumps and channels to carry water away, but ours had not been maintained. Andrew had noted all this before but the dry surface was terribly hard and who wanted to go digging up a road in the Spanish summer? It was one of those jobs he put off. Now it was urgent because the edge of the track was disappearing before his eyes.

Water had softened the ground. He humped heavy stones, dumping them in the widening and deepening gap. The water streaming off hair and forehead was blinding. With large stones in place to arrest the erosion, he hacked channels to direct water away from the weak point. Once again the *azadon* proved itself the practical tool.

The next morning broke bright and sunny. There was a peculiar, unfamiliar noise, a sort of roar. Going to the edge of a terrace we gasped. The Rio Chico was flowing! Three or four inches had fallen but our soil had soaked it up. There were no puddles. We did not know whether this downpour reduced the risk of the spring running dry in the near future. The water we were taking might have fallen months or years before. As the hillside was porous limestone, we suspected it had fallen fairly recently. That was one reason we avoided drinking it: the spring was directly below the rubbish tip and higher still was the village with its cesspits.

There were plans to take rubbish to a central dump elsewhere in the area, but there were no indications of this happening. Not even after Manuel Chaves, prime minister of Andalusia, had visited the valley and insisted that the rubbish-tipping problems of the Alpujarra be cleared up.

The trouble was, only incomers considered it a problem. To the locals the suggestion was incomprehensible. Country people had always tipped their rubbish into the nearest *barranco* and did not understand why they should change the habit of centuries. The fact that there was a lot more rubbish, and that plastic and metal do not decay like cabbage leaves and potato peelings, did not impress them. Every few months they set fire to rubbish dumps and the air was foul with toxic fumes. No one could explain why they disregarded warnings about the dangers of poisonous smoke from low temperature burning of plastic.

At Carataunas some people were too lazy to walk to the chute and tossed their bags of rubbish anywhere along the track. Others dumped boxes which blew around or hardcore which bounded as far down as our pool. But when we met the mayor in the bar the only remedy he was willing to suggest was that we put up a 'No Tipping' sign. Even the prime minister could only urge, municipalities made their own arrangements.

A Spanish friend in Carataunas hated it too.

'But this is Spain,' said Andrew, meaning that Carataunas was not unique in its attitude.

'No, it is the mentality of the people here.' Our friend was from the north where they would not tolerate such filth.

Rubbish revealed a quirk in the Alpujarran mind. Houses and hotel rooms were usually spotless. There was little graffiti or litter. After a fiesta, streets were rapidly swept. English people renovating a village house made a terrible mistake by failing to whitewash their home before the fiesta. No one had told them it was expected, because it had not occurred to anyone that they did not know. So, appearances are extremely important.

And yet . . . those same people go into their bar and throw their sugar packets, paper napkins, olive stones, meat bones and cigarette ends on the floor. They see nothing offensive in that. Christine described the first time she and Philip were invited into a Spanish house for a meal. She ate an olive and could not see where to put the stone. She held it in her hand until she realized that all the detritus of the meal was being thrown to the floor.

Although rubbish on our track made us aware of every gusty day, we were spared most of the winds. They rampaged along the valley floor, hundreds of feet below us, raising dust in the streets of Órgiva. It was on one of these fairly typical Órgiva days that the woman was released from her tiny newspaper kiosk for an *obra*, building work. *El País* and *Ideal* leapt from her trestle table and tried to escape up the plaza. But soon she was rehoused, crammed into a slightly bigger kiosk, with more magazines and papers, yet still a Judy with no room for Mr Punch.

With her *obra* she followed a trend for renewal and expansion: new buildings in towns, new routes through the countryside. And with the new roads came new perspectives. Places are reckoned further apart, measured in car travel instead of footpaths. New views are opened up. One of our most memorable moments was driving back from Yegen, rounding a bend on a modern road and seeing the snow on the highest mountains luminous in the moonlight.

At Yegen, in late morning, we had sat in a simple bar, a whitewashed L-shaped room with a counter and a metal framed table. The owner broke off talking to his only customer to serve us. He was taciturn. You could almost hear him thinking: 'More ruddy tourists.' But we asked anyway. 'Are there other things in the village connected with Gerald Brenan, apart from his house?'

'No.'

He turned to resume the conversation, shutting us out. We finished our drinks and went into the square. No women gossiped around the fountain as they had in Brenan's day. Piped water changed all that.

A plaque identified the house where once lived 'the British Hispanicist who made universally known the name of Yegen and the customs and traditions of the Alpujarra'. Ceramic words were partly obscured by careless whitewashing. Modern windows had replaced his wooden shutters. Judging by appearances Yegen had mixed feelings. We knew it had been scandalized by his book.

South from Granada had come into our hands in an odd way, months before our first visit to Andalusia. Ill and delirious, Lesley had announced: 'I'm going to die before I see the Alhambra.' It wasn't something that interested her really, but while she was recuperating we planned the trip. Andrew was choosing maps in Marylebone High Street when she picked up a copy of Brenan's book and discovered the Alpujarra. The goal posts shifted, that was what she wanted to see. We fitted it all in. And went back and went back.

It is simplistic to say the Alpujarra has changed more in the sixty or so years since Brenan lived in Yegen than in the previous six hundred. No change could have been greater than the upheaval when the Moors were expelled. Yet in his time cars, telephones, gas and electricity had barely touched the area. There was a road above the village going in the Almeria direction but Órgiva could only be reached mounted or on foot.

To outward appearances, Yegen as we saw it was much the same as it used to be. A Cubist picture by Braque or a battered Le Corbusier style development, as Brenan variously described it. It has not grown. The striking difference is the colour. In the 1920s it was grey stone. Later it was perked up with white-

212

wash. We looked into the church. A very modern nun prayed in a corner. This was where the priest had obliged Brenan, a Protestant, to sit in the bishop's throne while the Latin Mass was intoned. Since then both building and services have been simplified, rearranged, made plain. The Alpujarra has also become accessible, no longer cut off by mountains, cliffs and gorges. Like the priest it now faces outwards.

Eduardo Castro, writing in 1992, said in the introduction to his extensive *Guide to the Alpujarra*:

'No one has, in effect, captured the singularity and beauty of the Alpujarra as Brenan has. So, if there is any writer linked with this region in an indelible way, it is him. His descriptions of the geography, customs, folklore and history of the Alpujarra have the stamp of his excellence as a narrator. Without his work, the image of the Alpujarra today would be very different.'

Exactly! It is an image of the past. Visitors go to Yegen to seek out the quaint, but no community wants to be thought of as living in the past.

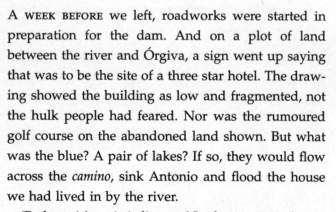

CHAPTER TWENTY-EIGHT
MUY PRECIOSA

A WEEK BEFORE we left, roadworks were started in preparation for the dam. And on a plot of land between the river and Órgiva, a sign went up saying that was to be the site of a three star hotel. The drawing showed the building as low and fragmented, not the hulk people had feared. Nor was the rumoured golf course on the abandoned land shown. But what was the blue? A pair of lakes? If so, they would flow across the *camino*, sink Antonio and flood the house we had lived in by the river.

'Perhaps it's artistic licence,' Lesley suggested.

'Perhaps they don't know the *camino*'s there. It isn't on any maps.'

We locked up Las Monjas for the last time, forgot to pick the figs we had promised ourselves, and steered the jeep on its final journey through the tricky hairpins. A flock of little kestrels, a dozen of them, circled overhead. A ragged old tabby from the village watched us go. Diego was hitching a lift down the hill but we had no room for him. He bade us goodbye with his usual elaborate courtesy. It was the weekend of the *retornados*.

We took the beautiful road west across the sierras. The sunflowers were being harvested, brittle brown heads gulped by machinery in fields of dull gold.

Turning north, we ticked off some of the places we had intended to visit sooner, if we had not become entranced with our olive trees and our oranges and the special pleasures nearer to hand. We went to Salamanca, where the university had once been closed because academics challenged the right of king and church to slaughter their way across South America. Then to Santiago de Compostela, and the great cathedral that set out to rival St Peter's in Rome. A priest cupped a hand to his ear and nearly fell out of the box in an effort to hear confession above the hubbub of tourists and pilgrims. We went to Covadonga where, in 718, or so the story goes, Pelayo won the first battle of the Reconquest. In the cave a priest was giving a spirited sermon about that misnomer: before the Moors there were only Visigoths and Romans; Pelayo took the first step in the march of Catholicism across Spain. Our minds flitted back to a pathetic ruin in Andalusia, the last toehold of a Moorish king.

'Where have you been?' wondered the receptionist at a smart hotel by a flashing river in Asturias.

Our jeep, crammed with home going oddments, was out of place.

'We've been living in the Alpujarra.'

She gave a little gasp of delight. *'Muy preciosa!'*

And so it is.

ACKNOWLEDGEMENTS

Our thanks go to all those who have shared with us their love and knowledge of the Alpujarra. Some are given their real names in this book while details of others have been changed to respect their wish for privacy. Many do not feature in this story although they were a part of our satisfying and enjoyable life there. *Muy gracias a todos*.

The books we have referred to and enjoyed include:

In English
South from Granada by Gerald Brenan (Cambridge University Press paperback 1980).
Handbook for Travellers in Spain by Richard Ford (William Murray, 1845 and subsequent editions).

Spanish Gardens by the Marquesa de Casa Valdés (Antique Collectors' Club, 1987).

A Guide to Andalusia by Michael Jacobs (Penguin, 1991).

Andalusia by Hugh Seymour-Davies and Charles Waite (George Philip, 1990).

The Spaniards by John Hooper (Penguin, 1987).

Cooking in Spain by Janet Mendel Searl (Lookout, 1987).

Lorca's Granada by Ian Gibson (Faber and Faber, 1992)

IN SPANISH

Guia General de la Alpujarra by Eduardo Castro (La General, Granada, 1992).

La Alpujarra (Two vols) by Miguel J Carrascosa Salas (Universidad de Granada, 1992).

Andar por la Alpujarra by Augustín García Martínez and others (Accion Divulgativa, Madrid, 1992).

Mil ochenta recetas de cocina by Simone Ortega (Alianza Editorial, Madrid, 1972).